MAKING OLD-FASHIONED
SANTAS

Candie Frankel
& Beverly Karcher

Sterling Publishing Co., Inc. New York

For Dick and Fred

The Victorian Net Santas, page 70, were originally featured in
McCall's Needlework and Crafts October 1989 issue
and are presented here by permission.

Library of Congress Cataloging-in-Publication Data Available

1   3   5   7   9   10   8   6   4   2

First paperback edition published in 1995 by
Sterling Publishing Company, Inc.
387 Park Avenue South, New York, N.Y. 10016
© 1994 by Candie Frankel & Beverly Karcher
Distributed in Canada by Sterling Publishing
⅝ Canadian Manda Group, One Atlantic Avenue, Suite 105
Toronto, Ontario, Canada M6K 3E7
Distributed in Great Britain and Europe by Cassell PLC
Wellington House, 125 Strand, London WC2R 0BB, England
Distributed in Australia by Capricorn Link (Australia) Pty Ltd.
P.O. Box 6651, Baulkham Hills, Business Centre, NSW 2153, Australia
Printed and bound in Hong Kong
All rights reserved

Sterling ISBN 0-8069-8818-5 Trade
0-8069-8819-3 Paper

CONTENTS

ACKNOWLEDGMENTS

It is with deep appreciation and fondness that we credit the talented people who contributed to this book. Eileen Lane and her contagious enthusiasm inspired the confidence to get started, and Rosemary Gabriel Maceiras, who brought us together in an earlier project, suggested our collaboration once again. The book's real beginnings, though, go back to Cheryl Sentivan, who opened the door for us to the collector's world of antique chocolate moulds. Anne De Almeida acted as unofficial mould scout, Betty Vandewater painted the moulded chalkware, and Barbara Merola showed us how to turn out perfect chocolate Santas. For performing countless behind-the-scenes tasks, from stringing beaded stars to pouring hard candy suckers, we sing the praises of Betty Kiyler—she brought us joy, laughter, and perspective, along with willing hands.

On the technical side, we are indebted to Philip Karcher, Ed Noriega, and Ken Vandewater for their time and expertise "computerizing" our patterns and diagrams; to Lynne Vandewater, who critiqued the manuscript and made valuable suggestions; and to Steve Gross and Susan Daley, for their unpressured approach, close teamwork, and beautiful photography.

Most authors save their final mention for their immediate families, and we are no exception. Our heartfelt thanks to Philip, David, and Rebecca Karcher, and especially to Dick Karcher and Fred Frankel, for living with, around, and under Santa Claus for three years running. Your patience, your support, and your love are beyond measure.

INTRODUCTION

Just a little over a century ago, to celebrate Christmas was to savor the smallest delight. Many of those delights—simple ornaments and decorations—were made at home by resourceful mothers, grandmothers, and aunts, using materials bought in five-and-ten-cent stores. As America entered the 1900s, these same neighborhood stores stocked items supplied by Germany's cottage ornament industry and later by the factories of post–World War I Japan. Christmas decorations are notoriously fragile, and those that have survived are today eagerly sought by collectors (at handsome prices).

This book will show you how to re-create old-time Santa Claus figures, angels, and other Christmas decorations and ornaments. The collection spans a seventy-year time period, from the 1860s through the Great Depression. Each project is based on a historic original but can be made using contemporary techniques and new or recycled materials. You will probably want to scout out some vintage fabrics and findings for some of your Santas. Each project features step-by-step directions, and all the patterns are actual-size, ready to trace and use. Invite the entire family or a group of friends to participate; everyone can contribute, and adults can help youngsters acquire new skills, from pinching the clamps on a chocolate mould to operating a sewing machine.

The rewards of making, rather than buying, holiday decorations range from greater self-expression to plain old-fashioned thrift. The projects in this book would be expensive indeed were you to purchase them at an artist's market. But we hope you have opened these pages not simply to save money. Devoting your time and attention to a craft project can help you unwind, relax, and collect your thoughts—especially important dividends during the busy holiday season. More and more households across America are retreating from the excesses of the holidays and are making a conscious effort to stop consuming and start creating. As nineteenth-century homemakers knew, it is good for the soul.

CRAFTER'S NOTES

The projects presented here call for a variety of basic craft and sewing skills. These include working with modelling compound, painting, scoring, stringing beads on wire, using hand tools such as drills and saws, and cutting out and sewing simple patterns. If a particular medium or tool is new to you, follow the project directions closely. If you have questions, consult a knowledgeable family member or friend for guidance. *Always observe the correct safety procedures when using sharp blades or handling electrical tools.*

Although the projects may look involved, they are all easy and fun to make. Some of them can be completed in a few minutes, while others will have you engrossed for hours. The more complex projects can easily be broken down into several smaller segments.

BEFORE YOU BEGIN

When you first choose a project to make, read through the directions so that you have a basic grasp of how the project is assembled. Gather the materials and tools you will need, and note any missing items that you will have to buy or borrow before you can begin. In addition to the tools and supplies listed, you will also need a sewing machine (for some projects), hand-sewing needles, pins, sewing shears, sharp scissors (for cutting paper and cardboard), tracing paper, transparent tape, pencils, and a ruler.

Decide where you will work on

your project. A specially dedicated craft area is ideal. A simple setup—such as a small table in a corner of a room—will allow you to keep work in progress out in the open so that you can take advantage of small blocks of time that pop up in your schedule. Make sure your work area is well lit, preferably by a flexible tensor lamp that can be maneuvered into a variety of positions. If space is tight and your work area must be shared with other activities, store all your project materials in a tote bin so that you have what you need at your fingertips and can set up and clean up quickly.

TOOLS, SUPPLIES, AND MATERIALS

Always use the tool recommended in the project directions. Examples include pliers with a built-in wire cutter (for bending and cutting wire), a drill with specific-sized bits, a hot-glue gun, and assorted brushes. Using the incorrect tool may hamper your project results, compromise your safety, or damage your tools.

Supplies such as glue and paint should also be chosen following the project directions. Use clear arts-and-crafts glue to bond paper and cardboard. Use thick white tacky glue to bond hard-to-hold surfaces or surfaces that differ in texture or composition. A glue applicator with a slender curved tip lets you apply glue in a fine bead and direct small dots of glue into tight or awkward areas. When a glue applicator is not

specified, spread the glue evenly across the surface with a stiff brush. For an extra-strong bond, use a glue gun.

The materials listed for each project include fabric, fur, thread, trims, beads, foil, scraps, dowels, and other items. Pay close attention to dimensions and quantities when selecting project materials, but feel free to introduce your own colors, textures, and personality into a project through the fabrics and findings you choose. Most of the project materials can be readily obtained at craft and hobby retailers, bakery supply stores, fabric stores, stationery stores, art supply stores, party supply stores, and hardware stores. Seasonal stores specializing in Christmas decorations are a good source for berry pips, pinecones, pine and tinsel stems, tree drapes, wrapping papers, and scraps. For vintage and one-of-a-kind fabrics, trims, beads, and other surprise finds, visit rummage sales and thrift shops.

PATTERNS AND DIAGRAMS

All of the patterns for the projects are printed actual-size. To copy a pattern, lay a sheet of tracing paper over it and trace the pattern lines with a pencil. To use a pattern tracing, pin or tape it to fabric, paper, or wood as directed in the project steps and cut out the final version. To protect the book pages during tracing, lay a sheet of clear acetate on the pattern page and lay the tracing paper on top. Slide the

edges of both sheets into the book gutter to prevent slipping, and then trace as usual.

Sew all fabric seams 1/4" from the edge and all felt seams 1/8" from the edge using a matching color thread. The appropriate seam allowance is indicated on the patterns. Some project pieces are sewn from squares or rectangles of fabric. The dimensions for these pieces are specified in the project directions and include the required seam allowances. Some projects feature special cutting diagrams, which also include seam allowances.

A FINAL WORD

Old-fashioned Christmas ornaments and decorations are appealing because they are individualistic. When you make the Santas and other decorations in this book, you can follow the directions precisely for projects that will look like those shown in the photographs, or you can explore each project's possibilities using the fabrics, trims, and accessories of your choosing. The latter course is adventurous and fun, and if you are not inclined to branch out on your own, we encourage you to try.

BELSNICKELS &
SANTA FIGURES

❉ ❉ ❉ ❉ ❉ ❉ ❉ ❉

The serious, demanding-looking Santas made one hundred years ago are always a bit startling to the modern eye. Today Santa is jolly and red-cheeked, not above proffering a telling wink to let folks know the gift is in the bag. Most of yesteryear's St. Nicks were made of sterner stuff. Curious and reclusive, they wandered about the countryside in long, funny coats distributing evergreens and fruit to the poor. Many wore a perpetual scowl; some carried switches; gifts were by no means guaranteed. So formidable was St. Nick in young imaginations that mothers reported their children more polite, considerate, and less prone to bickering during the Advent season.

The dual-personality Santa, who both rewards good and punishes evil, grew out of Reformation-era sensibilities. To downplay the popular influence of the saints, Protestant sympathizers demoted St. Nicholas, the legendary fourth-century bishop, from his traditional gift-giving role. He became Father Christmas in England and Weihnachtsmann—the Christmas man— in Germany. St. Nicholas lingered on in German popular culture as Pelze-Nichol, or Belsnickel, which means fur-clad Nicholas.

In one tradition, the gifts were delivered by Christkind—the Christ child—and Pelze-Nichol trailed along behind, keeping track of everyone's sins.

Santa Claus figures of moulded chocolate, chalkware, and papier-mâché made for late nineteenth-century American markets were strongly influenced by Dutch and German traditions. Seventeenth-century Dutch Protestants continued to embrace the traditional St. Nicholas, whom they called Sinter Klaus. Later German immigrants bubbled over with enthusiasm for Christmas, putting up trees, exchanging gifts, and importing decorations and trinkets from Europe. Their festivities eventually won over American Protestants, who had previously viewed the holiday revelry—and Santa Claus—with raised eyebrows.

The projects featured in this section were among the first Santas displayed or sold commercially. They played a role in making Santa Claus a universally beloved secular figure. Poised on the cusp of a new merchandising age, they helped shape the American Christmas of today, even as they embraced the essence of Christmases past.

OLD-WORLD FATHER CHRISTMAS

Victorian penny magazines and greeting cards depicted Father Christmas as a sad, doleful soul. He wore rich fur pelts and a crown of holly around his head. Here, he carries a white lamb, an evergreen, and a candle—reminders of ancient as well as Christian traditions. His small hand basket is laden with nuts, berries, and pinecones. The pocket-sized book entitled Old Christmas *was a serendipitous find in a forgotten corner of an old house; you're sure to turn up your own treasures at flea markets, thrift shops, and rummage sales. The figure stands about 16" tall; a purchased doll stand is necessary to hold it upright.*

✳ ✳ ✳ ✳ ✳

MATERIALS AND TOOLS

6″ × 12″ Osnaburg fabric

15″ × 30″ burgundy heavy wool fabric

15″ × 30″ printed challis

18″ × 18″ light brown wool fabric

10″ × 12″ dark brown wool fabric

tan pearl cotton, size 3

ecru heavy-duty sewing thread

batting strips

fiberfill

one 12″ braid white wool doll hair

two rabbit hair pelts

⅝″ × 24″ leather strip

lamb ornament, about 4″ long

6″ bottlebrush tree

small basket, about 2″ across

assorted small pinecones, nuts, berries, and pine stems

candle in metal candle holder (counter-balance type, for use on Christmas tree)

assorted pips, berries, and leaves on wire stems

two 16″ lengths of ⅞″ dowel

wire coat hanger

thick rubber band

black, blue, rose, and white acrylic fabric paints

black fine-tip permanent pen

nonaerosol hair spray

thick white tacky glue

hot-glue gun

crewel needle

3½″ doll-making needle

medium and fine paintbrushes

stiff brush (for glue)

small scissors or new single-edge razor blade

compass

needle-nose pliers

heavy-duty wire cutters

drill with ⅛″ bit

vise

doll stand for 16″–18″ doll

DIRECTIONS

1. Trace the actual-size boot and sole patterns. Cut out four boots (reverse two) and two soles from dark brown wool fabric. Place boots together in pairs, wrong sides facing, and machine-stitch front and back seams. Ease in soles by hand, matching dots; leave tops open. Turn boots to right side.

2. Cut two 6″ × 8″ pants legs and one 10″ × 16″ tunic from light brown wool fabric. Fold each piece in half, right side in and shorter edges matching. Sew shorter edges together to make a tube. Turn right side out.

TO MAKE THE LEGS:

3. Mark a dot on each dowel 2″ from one end. Secure each dowel in a vise for drilling. Using a ⅛″ bit, drill a hole straight through the dowel on the marked dot.

4. Stuff fiberfill firmly into the toe of one boot. Apply hot glue to the undrilled end of one dowel, and lower it into the boot. Position the dowel so that the drilled hole runs from side to side; then press the dowel down against the inside heel. Pack additional fiberfill solidly around the dowel to support it in an upright position. Repeat for other boot.

5. Cut a 48″ length of tan pearl cotton. Fold it in half and thread the doubled length through a crewel needle. Following the number order shown in Diagram 1, "sew" lacing across the front seam of boot. Tie ends at the outside top and let them fall to the side. Repeat for other boot.

6. Using matching thread, sew a running stitch around the raw edges of both pants legs. Slip a pants leg over a dowel—make sure the inseam faces in—and pull the lower basting threads to gather the edge tightly around top of boot. Tie thread ends securely. Hand-sew gathered edge to boot. Stuff fiberfill lightly through the top, gather closed, and tie off. Repeat for second leg.

7. Mark two 1″ × 6″ cuffs on wrong side of one fur pelt; hair growth should be towards longer

The pants leg hem is hand-gathered and tacked to the boot (Step 6). Fur cuffs will conceal the stitching.

BOOT TOP

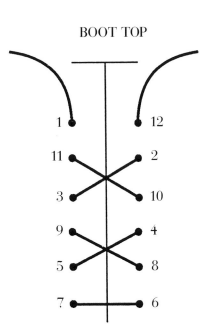

Diagram 1

edge. Cut out from wrong side with small scissors or a new single-edge razor blade, carefully separating the hairs so that you cut the skin only. Arrange a cuff around each ankle so that hair growth points down. Glue in position with tacky glue, concealing raw edges where boot and pants leg meet.

Note: Support the armature in the doll stand for the remaining steps.

TO MAKE THE TUNIC:

8. Using matching thread, sew a running stitch around the raw edges of the tunic. Hold the legs together so that both boot toes point forward and the drilled holes align from side to side. Secure the dowels 1″ from the top with a rubber band. Slip the tunic over the dowels, covering top of pants legs. Pull the lower tunic basting threads to gather the edge snugly around upper pants. Stuff fiberfill gently into the tunic through the top to fill out figure;

then tighten the top gathering threads and tie off the ends. Tie leather strip below belly to conceal join.

TO MAKE THE ARMS:

9. Using the wire cutters, snip the top off the wire hanger and discard (Diagram 2). Unbend the wire; it should be about 36″ long. Slip the wire through the two drilled holes so that an equal length extends on each side. Wrap each extension once around both dowels to secure the join and draw tight.

Note: Any sturdy, bendable wire can be substituted for the coat hanger wire. One suggestion is flat vinyl-coated electrical wire, which can be wrapped directly around the dowels without predrilling. It is sold by the foot in hardware stores in some areas. You will need 3 feet.

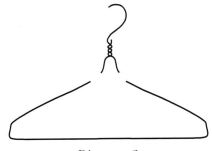

Diagram 2

10. Remove the rubber band, and hot-glue the dowels together 1″ from the top. Bend each wire arm into a 1″ loop 8″ from the dowel to form a hand. Twist wire with pliers to secure the loop, and clip off excess. Cut two 1¼″ × 18″ strips of batting. Wrap strips around arms and hands to pad them, and secure with tacky glue.

Loop "hands" are fashioned at each end of the coat hanger armature (Step 10).

11. Trace the actual-size mitten pattern. Cut four mittens (reverse two) from light brown wool. Place mittens together in pairs, right sides facing, and sew curved seams; leave wrists open. Stitch again over previous stitching to reinforce thumb. Clip curves and turn to right side. Slip onto padded wire hands, and tack or glue at wrist.

TO MAKE THE HEAD:

12. Using a compass, draft a 5″-diameter circle on tracing paper for head pattern. Cut two heads from Osnaburg fabric. Fold each head circle in half, right side in. Sew a gently curving seam along each fold, about ½″ near the edges and tapering to ³⁄₁₆″ in the middle (Diagram 3).

13. Open up the head circles and place them together, right sides facing and seams matching. Sew all around, leaving a 2″ neck opening at base of vertical seam (Diagram 4).

14. Turn head right side out. Stuff firmly, shaping so that vertical seams run down middle of head

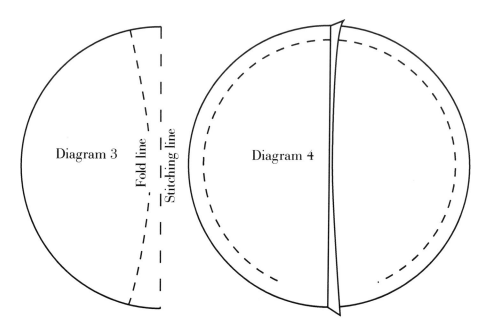

Diagram 3 · Fold line · Stitching line

Diagram 4

neck opening touches top of padded wire shoulders. Use a chopstick to stuff additional fiberfill through neck opening if necessary. Sew a running stitch around neck opening and gather closed.

TO PAINT THE EYES:

18. Paint a white almond shape below each sculpted eyebrow. (If you feel uncomfortable painting

A chopstick helps maneuver fiberfill into position inside the head (Step 17).

front and back. Divide the face horizontally into thirds, and mark with basting thread.

TO SCULPT THE NOSE:

15. Thread a 3½″ doll-making needle with heavy-duty ecru thread and knot the thread end. Pinch the middle third of the vertical seam with your fingers to form nose. Insert the needle into the neck opening and draw it out at the top of the nose, catching the knot in the fiberfill. Sew small ⅛″ running stitches down the seamline, pulling the thread gently but firmly to raise the Osnaburg fabric into a ridge (you should catch some of the fiberfill underneath as you sew). Continue working until stitching reaches the bottom third of the face and end off. You can make the nose broader at the bottom if you wish.

TO SCULPT THE EYES:

16. Pinch the fabric to left and right of the bridge of the nose to create eyelid ridges. Manipulate

each ridge with your fingers into a curve, and sew as for nose. Take additional stitches underneath the eye area to shape lower-eye curve (carry the thread on the wrong side to reach this area). Remove basting threads.

TO ATTACH THE HEAD:

17. Place the head on the dowels, manipulating fiberfill so that dowels are firmly lodged inside head and

Tiny hand stitches create the sculpted face details (Steps 15 and 16).

freehand, draw the almonds lightly first with a pencil.) Let dry; then paint a blue circle inside each almond for an iris. Visualize the iris as a clock face. While blue paint is still wet, apply three black streaks at the 1 o'clock position and blend in softly. Add a dot of white at the 1 o'clock position and a small white arc between 7 o'clock and 9 o'clock. Shade eyelid and under-eye area with light pink (mix rose and white paints). Outline the entire eye, and draw in lashes with a black fine-tip permanent pen. Brush rose paint on cheeks to blush them.

FACE-PAINTING TIPS

❋ Select quality acrylic paints designed for craft use on fabric, paper, wood, or plaster.

❋ Keep several sizes of soft brushes on hand so that you can try out different techniques. Be sure to wash out your brushes in cool water between colors while paint is still wet.

❋ If you have never painted a face before, practise first on scrap paper. You can create several sample faces and hold them up to your Santa to see which expression you like best.

❋ If your brush strokes are a bit wobbly, try resting your elbow on the tabletop to steady your hand as you work.

❋ To finish the face, dust on powdered makeup and fix with a light protective layer of nonaerosol hair spray.

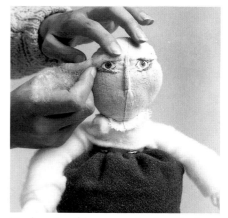

Wool roving fibres are glued to the face to create the eyebrows, moustache, and beard (Step 23).

TO MAKE THE COAT AND HOOD:

19. Trace the actual-size patterns for coat front and coat back. Cut two coat fronts (reverse one) and one coat back from burgundy wool. Cut matching pieces from challis for lining.

20. Place coat fronts against coat back, right sides facing and edges matching. Stitch shoulder and side/underarm seams. Repeat to assemble lining. Turn coat right side out. Place lining over it, right sides facing. Sew lining to coat along outer and neck edges; leave wrists open. Clip curves, turn to right side, and edge-stitch.

21. Cut a 4½″ × 10½″ piece of burgundy wool for hood. Fold in half crosswise, and sew one 5¼″ edge; turn.

22. Place coat on figure, easing arms through sleeves. Place hood on head. Cut two 1″ × 7″ cuffs and one 1″ × 10½″ hood trim from fur as for boot cuffs (Step 7). Glue cuffs around each wrist so that hair growth points down and raw sleeve edges are concealed. Glue trim around hood edge to frame face. Arrange remaining rabbit pelt around shoulder for cape and glue in place. Hood can be adjusted to fall inside or outside of cape at back.

TO ATTACH THE BEARD:

23. Cut the 12″ wool braid in two, for one 10″ and one 2″ length. Unbraid the 10″ piece, fold it in half, and tack it to the face just below the nose. Fluff up the fibres with a pin. Unbraid the 2″ piece, separate out a small lock, and tack just below the nose for a long moustache. Tuck small tufts of remaining beard wool under hood for hair. Glue small tufts to face for eyebrows. Fix all hair lightly with hair spray.

FINISHING AND TRIMS:

24. Squirt hot glue into basket and arrange assorted nuts, pinecones, berries, and pine stems inside. Add more glue as necessary.

25. Bend arms up at elbows to hold gifts. The figure shown carries a book with his left arm and a lamb, a tree, and some sprigs with pips in his right arm. A candle holder is lodged between the thumb and hand of the left mitten, and the basket is suspended from a cord that is looped over the right mitten. You can bend the mittens and arms to support the props you choose for your Father Christmas.

26. Wind berry and leaf stems into a 3″ to 4″ wreath, fill out with extra berries and leaves, and set on hood.

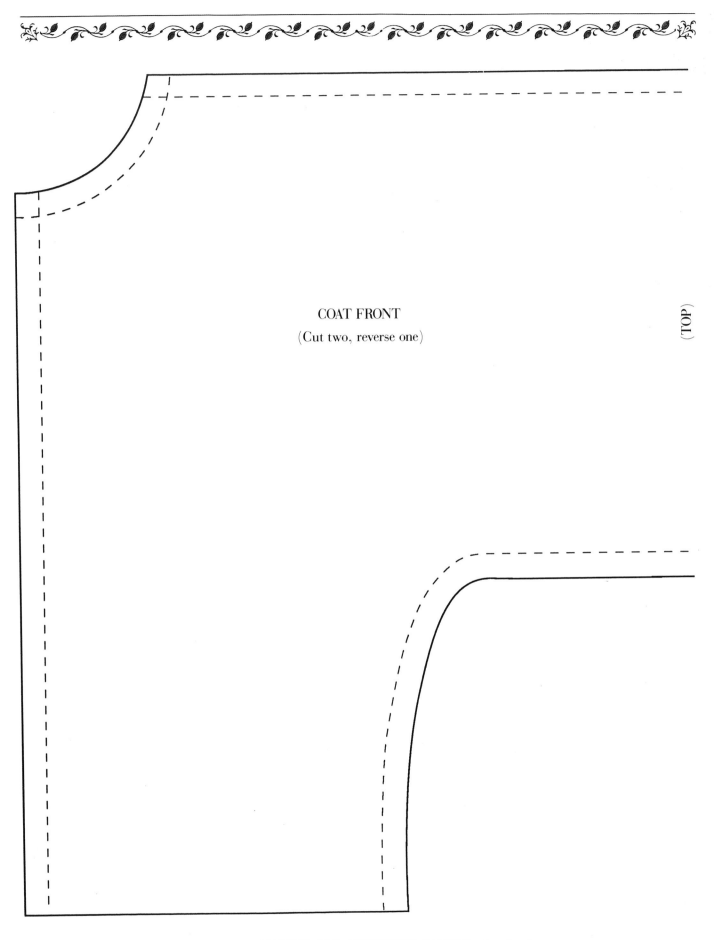

COAT FRONT

(Cut two, reverse one)

(TOP)

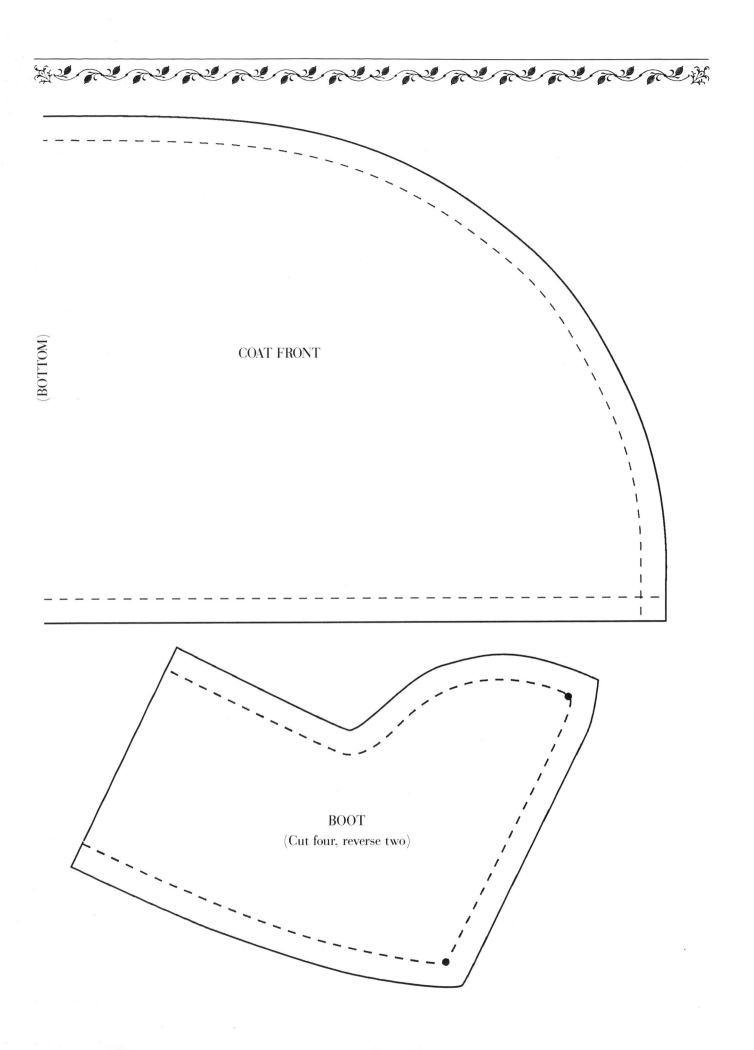

(BOTTOM)

COAT FRONT

BOOT
(Cut four, reverse two)

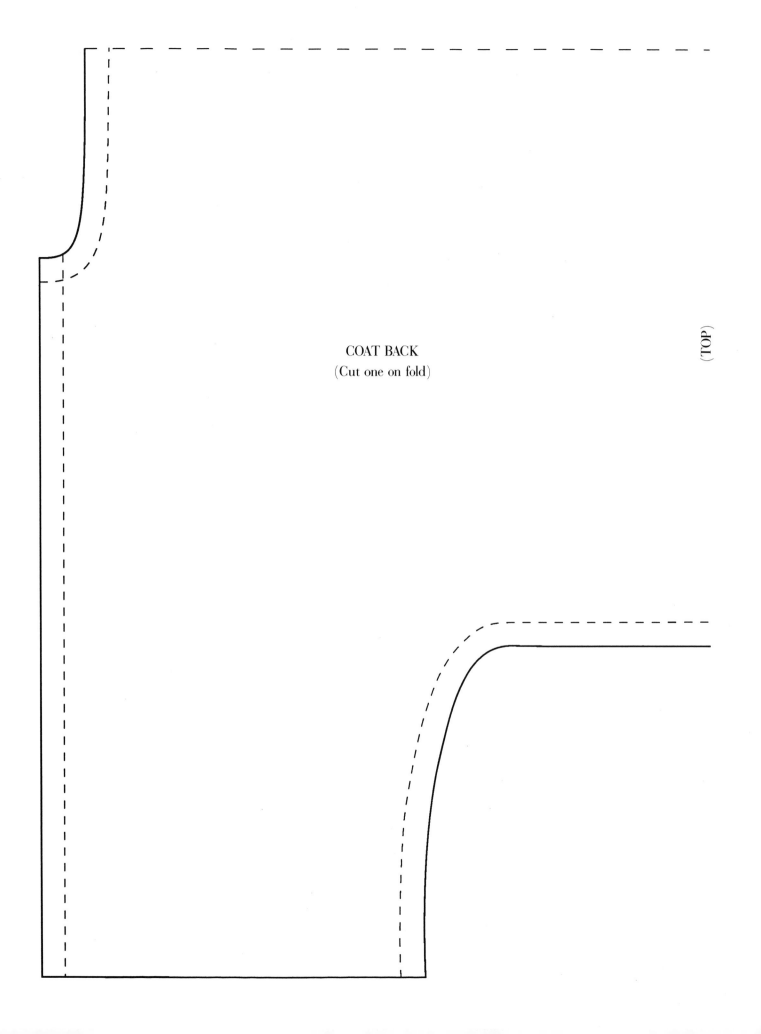

COAT BACK
(Cut one on fold)

(TOP)

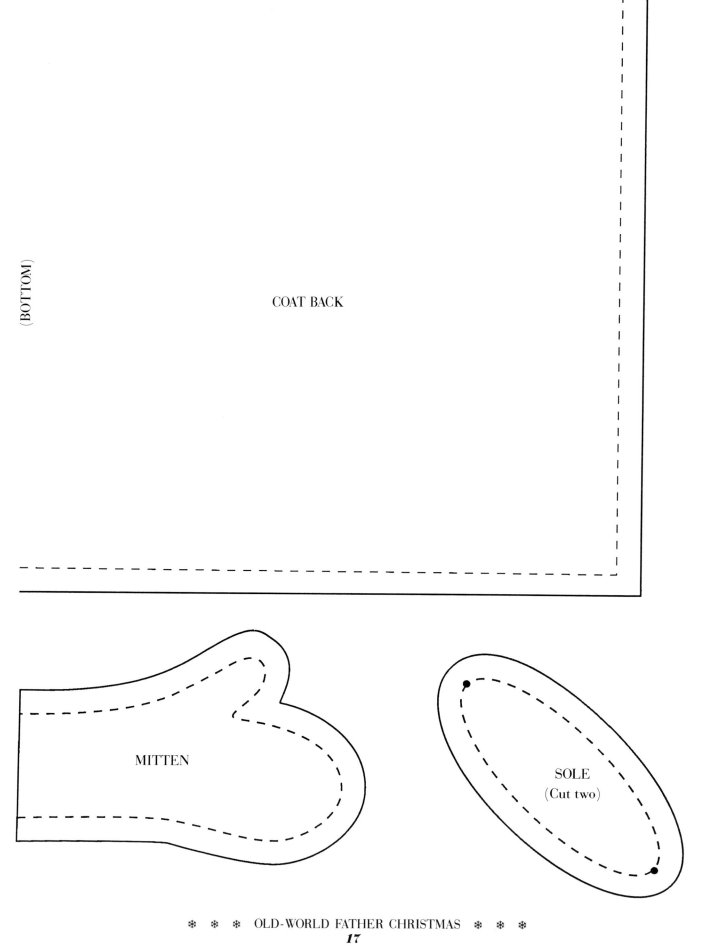

(BOTTOM)

COAT BACK

MITTEN

SOLE
(Cut two)

VICTORIAN BELSNICKEL

Often made in Germany, Belsnickels like this one decorated American shop windows as well as homes during Christmastime. The Belsnickel was grumpy, and Victorian children took seriously his reputation for leaving lumps of coal instead of candies and treats in their Christmas stockings. The faces of many antique Belsnickels were moulded of papier-mâché or plaster, but this version lets you try your hand with a contemporary modelling compound. The figure stands about 17" tall.

✳ ✳ ✳ ✳

MATERIALS AND TOOLS FOR THE HEAD, HANDS, AND BOOTS

1 lb. modelling compound

2½″ Styrofoam egg

five 18″ stems of 18-gauge florist's wire

black, blue, Caucasian skin tone, red, rose, and white acrylic paints

water-based antique finish

water-based clear matte finish

medium and fine paintbrushes

pencil with eraser tip

toothpick

wire cutters

clay modelling tools (optional)

oven

baking rack

DIRECTIONS FOR THE HEAD, HANDS, AND BOOTS

1. Bend each 18″ florist's wire stem in half to form a hairpin shape.

TO MAKE THE HEAD:

2. Insert the two straight ends of one "hairpin" into the broad end of the Styrofoam egg. Push the wire ends down through the egg and out the other end. Measure a 1½″ extension, and cut off the excess.

3. Cover the egg with a ⅛″ layer of modelling compound, moulding it with your fingertips to make the surface as smooth as you can. Select the smoothest view of the egg for the face, and mentally divide it into horizontal thirds.

A layer of modelling compound smoothed over a Styrofoam egg forms the base for the head (Step 3).

TO MOULD THE NOSE:

4. Roll a pea-sized piece of modelling compound into a ball; then roll the ball into a ⅞″-long "sausage." Position the sausage vertically in the middle third of the face. Use your fingertips to gently mould the side and top edges into the surface to form a nose.

TO MOULD THE CHEEKS:

5. Shape two small "jellybeans." Position them on the face at each side of the nose, and mould the edges into the surface.

TO ADD THE EYES AND EYEBROWS:

6. Using the eraser end of a pencil, indent the face on each side of the bridge of the nose. Further define the eye sockets by pressing the outline with the end of a toothpick. Roll a pea-sized ball, divide it in half, and reroll each piece. Press each tiny ball into an eye socket, and flatten.

7. Roll two pea-sized balls into sausages. Press each sausage above an eye, arching it slightly. Mould the edges into the face, as for the nose. Use a toothpick to feather the edges, creating the look of hair.

Facial features are moulded from simple pea and sausage shapes (Steps 4–7).

Each addition is carefully smoothed into place. Eyebrows were feathered with the end of a toothpick (Steps 7 and 8).

TO MAKE THE MOUTH:

8. Roll one pea-sized ball, and flatten it slightly. Mould it onto the face below the nose, and indent the middle to form lips.

TO MAKE THE HANDS:

9. Roll a walnut-sized ball into a short sausage about 2½″ long. Slightly flatten two-thirds of the sausage to form a hand. Compress the remaining third evenly all around to suggest a wrist.

10. Roll one pea-sized ball into a sausage. Press it against the flattened hand section for a thumb and mould in the edges. Use a toothpick to indent three lines on the hand to suggest four fingers. Repeat Steps 9 and 10 to make another hand, making sure to reverse the thumb position.

11. Gently cup the fingers of the left hand. Shape the right hand into a tight fist. Use a toothpick to poke a hole through the middle of the fist to hold the tree stem.

12. Insert the two straight ends of a wire "hairpin" into the wrist end of each hand for about 1″.

TO MAKE THE BOOTS:

13. Roll two plum-sized balls. Mould each one into an L-shaped boot about 2½″ long, 2½″ high, and 1″ thick.

14. Insert the two remaining "hairpins" into the sole of each boot. Push through so that the wire ends come out the top of the boot and the hairpin bend lodges in the sole. Smooth extra modelling compound on sole to conceal the wire entry. Press in on the "arch"

of the foot with a straight-edged sculpting tool to form the boot heel.

Florist's wire is embedded in hands and boots before baking. The boot heel is shaped with a flat sculpting tool (Steps 12 and 14).

TO BAKE THE PIECES:

15. Bake the head, hands, and boots immediately in a 275°F (135°C) oven for 20 minutes, or as suggested in the modelling compound package instructions. Set on a rack until cool.

TO PAINT THE PIECES:

16. Paint all the pieces with acrylic paints. If you find you need to apply two coats for good coverage, be sure to let the paint dry between coats. Wash out the brush promptly in cool water when you change colors; do not let the paint harden on the brush. First, paint the hands and face Caucasian skin tone. Paint the boots black. When the face color is dry, paint the lips red. Brush rose paint on cheeks to blush them. Paint the eyebrows and almond-shaped eyes white. Paint a large black circle inside each eye. Paint a

smaller blue circle within each black circle for an iris. While blue paint is still wet, add a dot of black to the middle of each iris. Lightly brush the black paint through the top right quarter of each iris to shade it. Let dry. Visualizing the iris as a clock face, add a small white dot at the 2 o'clock position. Finally, dip a fine brush into a mix of black and red paint and outline each eyelid.

17. Brush the face, hands, and boots with the antique finish. Immediately wipe off excess with a soft cloth. Brush all pieces with clear matte finish.

MATERIALS AND TOOLS FOR THE BODY AND COAT

completed head, hands, and boots (see previous directions)

14″ × 35″ brick red heavy wool coat fabric

11″ × 44″ dark blue cotton fabric

3″ × 20″ thin cotton batting

heavy-duty thread

fiberfill

8″ white wool roving

1½″ × 2½″ × 4″ pine block

5½″ × 5½″ × 1″ pine (for base)

10¾″ of ¼″ dowel

½ yard white cotton string

small tree with ornaments, about 5″ high

small twig basket, about 2″ across

miniature berries and greens

white sparkling glitter

white opaque glitter

thumbtacks

black and white acrylic paints

acrylic modelling paste

thick white tacky glue

clear arts-and-crafts glue

glue applicator (for tacky glue)

stiff brush (for glues)

drill with ½″, ¼″, and ⅛″ bits

vise

DIRECTIONS FOR THE BODY AND COAT

TO MAKE THE STAND:

1. Following Diagram 1, measure and mark five points on the top, front, side, and bottom of the 1½″ × 2½″ × 4″ pine block.

Secure the block in a vise for drilling. Drill a hole at each marked point, using the appropriate bit, as follows:

- Top: ⅛″ bit, 1″ deep
- Bottom: ¼″ bit, 1″ deep
- Front: ½″ bit, drill clear through
- Side: ½″ bit, drill clear through

2. Following Diagram 2, mark a point on the pine base. Drill a ½″-deep hole using the ¼″ bit.

3. Using the glue applicator, squirt a few drops of tacky glue into the ¼″-diameter holes in both pine pieces. Insert one end of the 10¾″ dowel into each hole, and hold until the glue is set.

4. Paint the edges of the base black. Brush the top of the base with several coats of modelling paste, and let it accumulate near the edges to resemble snow. Paint the top of the base white.

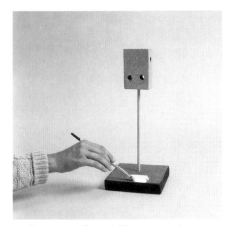

A first coat of modelling paste is applied to the base (Step 4).

TO MAKE THE ARMS AND LEGS:

5. Cut the blue cotton fabric into two strips, one 5″ wide (arms) and one 6″ wide (legs). Fold each strip in half lengthwise, right side in, and sew the long edges together, making ¼″ seams. Do not turn. Cut each strip in half, for two 22″ arms and two 22″ legs.

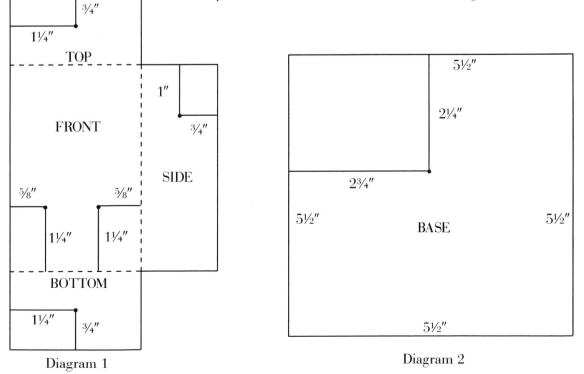

Diagram 1

Diagram 2

6. Insert a hand into one end of an arm so that the hand and wrist are concealed but the wire is visible. Apply a bead of tacky glue around the wrist. Gather the arm edge around the wrist, and tie heavy-duty thread around both. Turn the fabric arm right side out over the wire. Repeat for the second arm. Attach the boots to the legs in the same way.

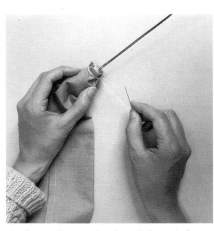

A sleeve edge is glued and then tied around the wrist for a secure join. When the sleeve is turned, all the raw edges fall to the inside (Step 6).

TO ATTACH THE ARMS AND LEGS:

7. Identify the right and left arms by the thumb position. Insert each arm wire through the appropriate side arm hole in the pine block. Allow about 3½″ of arm between the hole and the wrist (the fabric will bunch up around the wire). Bend the excess wire to the back, and secure with a thumbtack.

8. Stuff the lower (wire) end of each leg lightly with fiberfill. Insert the loose leg ends into the two leg holes at the front of the pine block.

Pull the leg fabric through to the back so that the wires just reach the holes and the boots rest on the base. Wrap the excess leg fabric around the block and tie in back.

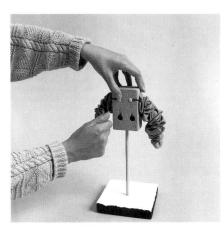

The fabric bunches together when the arm wires are drawn up, providing natural-looking bulk under the coat (Step 7).

TO ATTACH THE HEAD:

9. Squirt tacky glue into the top hole. Insert the double neck wire into the hole—about ½″ of wire should show, allowing you to tilt the head in a variety of positions.

TO MAKE THE COAT:

10. Trace the actual-size coat, cape, and hood patterns. From red wool fabric, cut one coat back (place pattern on fold), two coat fronts, one hood, and one cape.

11. Sew the coat fronts and back together at the shoulder/upper arm seams only. Lay the coat flat, right side up. Lay the cape on top, right side up, with the neck and straight front edges matching. Sew the neck and straight edges together, pivoting at the corners.

Excess leg fabric is wrapped around the body block, adding softness and fullness to the block form (Step 8).

12. Cut a 16″ length of red sewing thread. Hand-baste along the hood gathering line from the face edge to the dot and back again. Do not cut the loose thread end.

13. Sew the hood back seam. Pin the hood to the coat/cape, right sides facing and neck edges matching. Sew through all three layers ¼″ from the neck edge. Sew the side/underarm seams.

14. Put the coat on the doll form. Overlap the front flaps and secure the top with a long straight pin. Stuff a small amount of fiberfill into the hood to fill it out. Draw the loose ends of the basting thread to gather the hood into a soft curve. Turn the excess sleeve fabric to the inside and glue in place. Use scissors to trim the bottom of the coat if necessary—the hem should just cover the boot tops.

FINISHING AND TRIMS:

15. Cut the batting in half for two 1½″-wide strips. Fold each long edge ⅜″ to wrong side and steam-press. Secure the folds with a bead

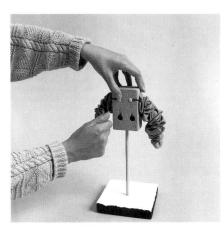

❄ ❄ ❄ MAKING OLD-FASHIONED SANTAS ❄ ❄ ❄

22

of tacky glue. Glue one strip around the edge of the cape, from one front edge to the other; trim off excess. Glue the second strip to the face edge of the hood, beginning at the neck. Continue this long strip down the front coat overlap. Trim off any excess.

16. Cut a 4″ length of white wool roving and glue it to the chin just below the lips for a beard. Cut two narrow 2″ to 3″ lengths, and glue the ends between the lips and nose for a moustache. Part the moustache to show the lips. Glue a small tuft above the forehead.

17. Bend Santa's right arm at the "elbow," and insert a tree into his fist. Make a gentle bend in the left arm, and slip a small basket over his arm. Tie white string around his waist and fray the ends.

18. Brush a thin coat of clear glue onto the top of the base, the top of the boots, and selected areas of the coat and hood. Sprinkle with white glitter "snow."

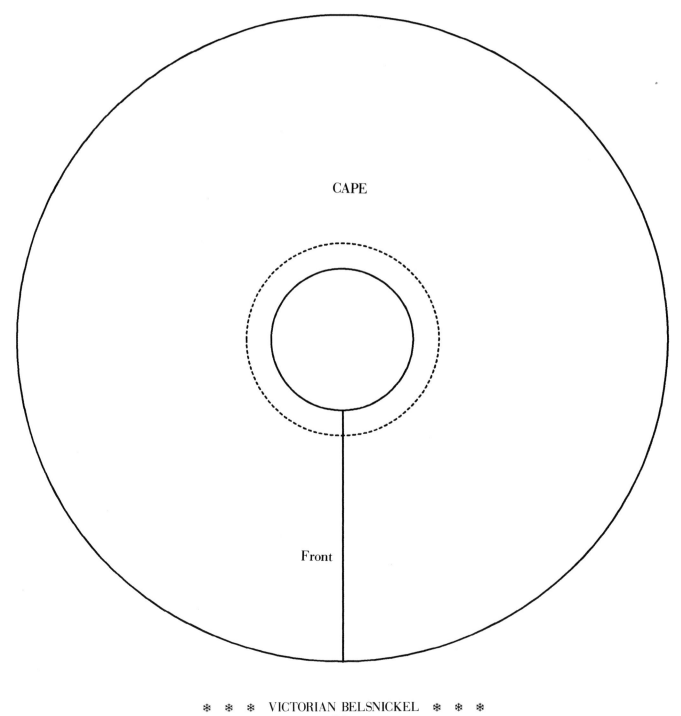

CAPE

Front

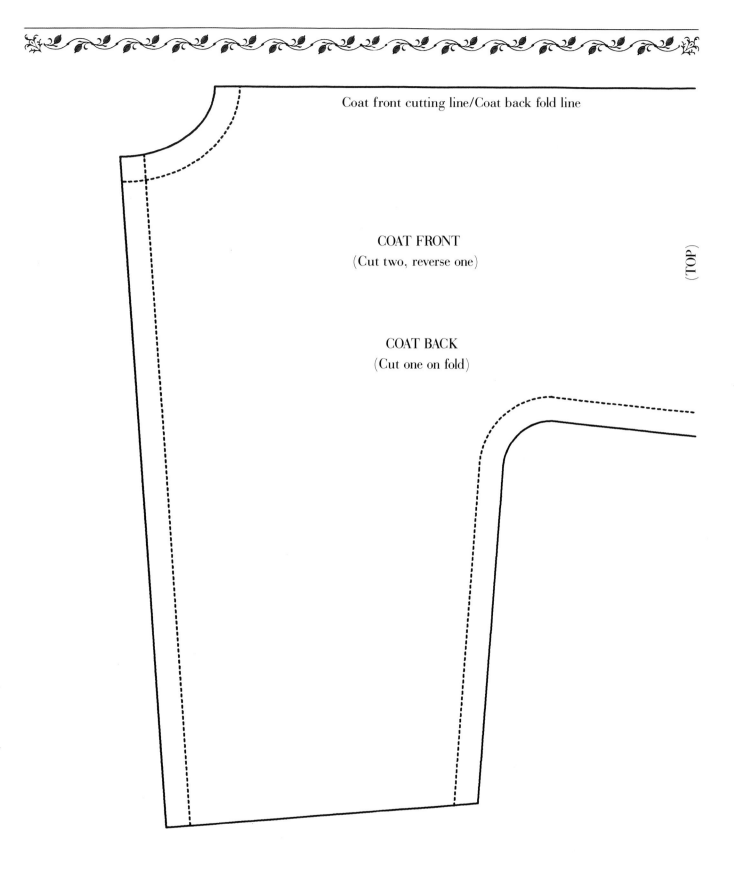

Coat front cutting line/Coat back fold line

COAT FRONT

(Cut two, reverse one)

COAT BACK

(Cut one on fold)

(TOP)

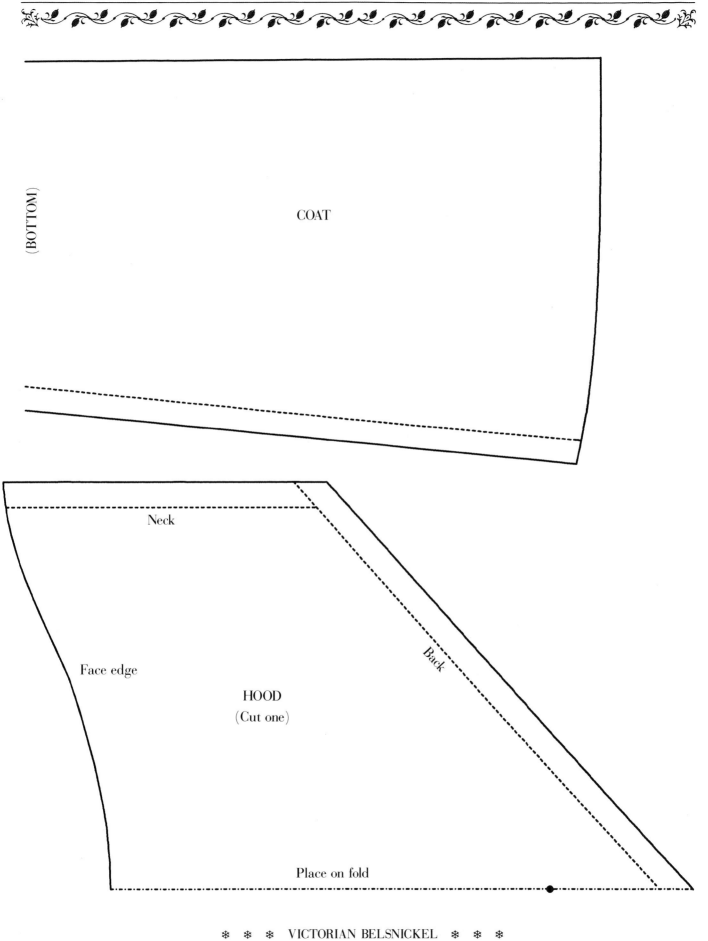

(BOTTOM)

COAT

Neck

Face edge

HOOD
(Cut one)

Back

Place on fold

CHALKWARE BELSNICKELS

*S*mall cast Belsnickels have been part of the German Christmas tradition since the late 1800s. The preferred medium was papier-mâché; the damp pulp was pressed into wooden moulds and allowed to dry. Some of these hollow pieces were subsequently dipped into liquid plaster, which dried to a smooth but unfortunately fragile shell. In America, the Pennsylvania Germans substituted plaster for papier-mâché, creating solid cast figures. Today, antique and reproduction metal chocolate moulds fill in for wooden moulds, and plaster is recommended over papier-mâché, as it sets up quickly and will not promote rust. The bright paint finish is traditional and accentuates the Belsnickels' fierce facial expressions. The figures shown are 4" to 8" tall.

✳ ✳ ✳ ✳ ✳

MATERIALS AND TOOLS

antique or reproduction metal chocolate Santa mould, two-piece with clamps, up to 8″ tall

plaster of paris

water

black, blue, Caucasian skin tone, gold, green, red, rose, and white acrylic paints

water-based antique finish

water-based matte finish

assorted paintbrushes, including extra-fine 10/0 size

olive oil in a spray bottle

reusable putty adhesive

liquid and dry measuring cups

glass or ceramic mixing bowl

tall wide-mouthed container

clean dishcloths or paper towels

spoon

paring knife

DIRECTIONS

TO MOULD BELSNICKEL:

1. Roll a piece of reusable putty adhesive into a long, skinny sausage. Lay it on the inside flange of one mould half, close to the impression. Press the mould halves together to create a seal. Fill the mould with water; then pour out the water into a liquid measuring cup. Add ¼ cup to the total for a small mould, ½ cup for a large mould.

2. Measure fresh water in this amount, and pour it into a clean

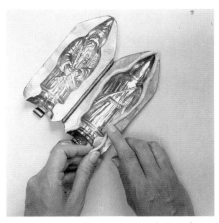

A thin band of putty around the edge creates a tight seal for measuring the mould's liquid volume (Step 1).

mixing bowl. Measure double this amount of dry plaster in the dry measuring cup, and add it to the water. Let sit 5 minutes so that the plaster can absorb the water.

3. While the plaster is setting, pry the mould apart and remove the putty. Wash both halves of the mould with warm, soapy water, rinse well, and dry thoroughly. Spray the inside of both halves lightly with olive oil. Clamp the halves together.

4. When the plaster is of a thick, soupy consistency, pour or spoon it into the mould in four stages. Tap the mould sharply against the side of a tabletop after each addition to settle the plaster. Set the upside-down mould in a tall container cushioned with clean dishcloths or paper towels so that it remains in a vertical position while the plaster is curing. The plaster will become hot as it cures, and then it will cool. The curing should take about an hour.

Note: Be sure to proceed to Step 5 promptly. Do not let the plaster cure

in the mould longer than an hour, or rust may form, particularly on antique moulds.

Add the mixed plaster in increments, tapping the mould sharply against the side of the table to settle the plaster into the mould. A tall container cushioned with paper towels keeps the mould in a vertical position as the plaster cures (Step 4).

5. As soon as the mould is cold to the touch, undo the clamps, remove one-half of the mould, and carefully pop out the figure. At this stage, the plaster will be firm but not yet bone-dry, giving you the opportunity to correct flaws. With a paring knife, carefully trim away any excess plaster that has collected at the seam. Run your finger firmly along the seam all around the figure to smooth the freshly trimmed edges. Stand the figure upright, test for wobbliness, and trim the underside of the base as necessary. If you see small holes on the surface, dip your finger in some of the chalky plaster you just trimmed off and run it lightly over the holes to fill them in. Use a soft dry brush to whisk off the excess. Allow the figure to dry

24 to 48 hours before painting (high humidity requires longer drying time).

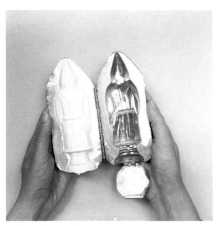

The plaster figure can be popped out when the mould is cold to the touch (Step 5).

TO PAINT BELSNICKEL:

6. Read the painting tips (see box that follows). Begin by painting the entire face the Caucasian skin tone, even areas that will be covered by other colors. Paint the eyebrows and

CHALKWARE PAINTING TIPS

❈ Paint in layers from the inside out—that is, paint the skin areas first, then facial features, then boots and coat, and, finally, anything that rests on top of the coat, such as a package, fur trim, or beard.

❈ If you find you need to apply two coats for good coverage, be sure to let the paint dry between coats.

❈ Wash out the brush in cool water whenever you change colors.

❈ Do not try to shade as you paint—shadowy effects will be produced by the antiquing finish.

almond-shaped eyes white. Paint a blue circle inside each eye for an iris. Visualizing the iris as a clock face, dip the tip of the narrow brush in white paint and add a white dot highlight at the 2 o'clock position. Use a fine brush and black paint mixed with red to outline the eyelids. Paint the lips rose. Don't be alarmed if your Belsnickel looks less than friendly—the originals could be quite mean-spirited!

7. Continue painting the figure's clothing and accessories, one color and layer at a time, until the entire surface is covered. Take your time and work carefully. Let dry overnight.

ANTIQUING AND FINISHING:

8. Dilute 1 part antiquing with 1 part water. Brush onto figure, allowing mixture to pool in crevices. Smooth out any noticeable drips with a dry brush. Let dry.

9. Brush entire figure with water-based matte finish. Work slowly so that bubbles don't form. Let dry thoroughly.

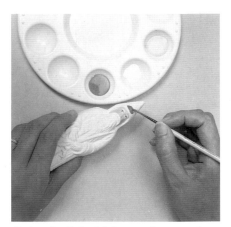

Paint the Belsnickel one color at a time. Allow each color to dry thoroughly before you introduce the next color (Steps 6 and 7).

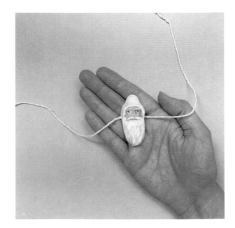

Painted plaster faces cast from chocolate moulds can add an authentic look to many projects, especially when you antique the surface and add a matte finish. The finished faces are glued in position or tied on with string that is embedded in the back of the casting when the plaster is still wet. Since the faces set up quickly, you can cast several in succession and then paint them as needed. For a look at some finished projects featuring plaster faces, turn to the Russian St. Nicholas, on page 35, the Victorian Net Santas, on page 70, the Japanese Net Santas, on page 75, and the Sailor Santa, on page 92.

MATERIALS AND TOOLS

antique or reproduction metal chocolate Santa mould, two-piece with clamps (see specific project directions for size)

plaster of paris

water

string or cord (see specific project directions for length)

black, blue, Caucasian skin tone, red, rose, and white acrylic paints

water-based antique finish

water-based matte finish

medium and fine paintbrushes

olive oil in a spray bottle

reusable putty adhesive

small glass bowl

measuring spoons

chopstick

DIRECTIONS

1. Wash the front half of the mould with warm, soapy water, rinse well, and dry thoroughly. Press a piece of reusable putty adhesive into the mould to seal off the face impression. Spay the inside of the face lightly with olive oil.

2. Measure 1 tablespoon of water into a small bowl. Add 2 tablespoons dry plaster. Let sit a few minutes until the plaster has absorbed the water. You can mix a larger amount for large moulds; keep the water/plaster ratio at 1:2.

3. When the plaster is of a thick, soupy consistency, spoon or pour it into the sectioned-off area of the mould. Drape the middle of the string into the wet plaster, and poke it beneath the surface with a chopstick. Let set for 10 minutes or until plaster cures.

4. When the mould is cold to the touch, remove the putty and pop out the plaster face. Let dry overnight. Finish with acrylic colors, antiquing, and matte finish; see To Paint Belsnickel and Chalkware Painting Tips opposite, for details.

Putty seals off the small face portion in a large Christmas tree mould (Step 1).

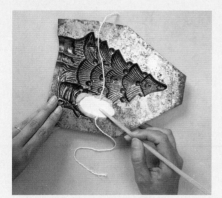

A chopstick helps sink the tie-on string into the wet plaster (Step 3).

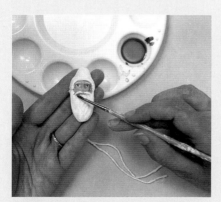

Water-based antiquing brushed onto the beard is allowed to pool in the crevices (Step 4).

CHOCOLATE SANTAS

MATERIALS AND TOOLS

antique or reproduction metal Santa chocolate moulds, two-piece with clamps or flat bars

confectioner's white, dark, or milk chocolate disks

two-cup Pyrex measuring cup

microwave oven

tall wide-mouthed container

clean dishcloths or paper towels

reusable putty adhesive

masking tape

ice-cream stick or toothpick

DIRECTIONS

1. Roll a piece of reusable putty adhesive into a long, skinny "sausage." Lay it on the inside flange of one mould half, close to the impression. Press the mould halves together to create a seal. Fill the mould with water, and then pour out the water into a measuring cup to determine the amount of chocolate you will need to melt. You can melt up to 12 oz. at a time in the microwave oven. For a bar mould, just fill mould with water and measure.

2. Pry the mould apart and remove

the putty. Wash both halves of the mould with warm, soapy water, rinse well, and dry thoroughly. Clamp the mould halves together; then mask edges with tape. Turn the mould upside down, and nestle it vertically inside a glass or jar cushioned with clean dishcloths or paper towels. Lay bar mould(s) wrong side up on a flat tray or baking dish.

3. Place 12 oz. of chocolate disks in a two-cup Pyrex measuring cup. Microwave for 60 seconds; then stir until disks are completely dissolved. If not completely dissolved after stirring, microwave for 10 seconds more and stir again. Repeat in 10-second blocks as necessary. Be careful not to overheat, which will cause streaking and discoloration.

4. Pour the hot liquid chocolate into the mould until full. Lift the mould out of its cushioning, and tap it sharply against the side or top of a table to bring the air bubbles to the surface. When air bubbles no longer appear on the surface, stand the mould back in its cushioning and refrigerate for 10 minutes or until set. When firm, undo the clamps and carefully remove one-half of the metal mould. Turn over and press gently to release the figure. To release chocolate from a bar mould, simply turn the mould over and press gently.

5. You can bring out the highlights of your mould by using contrasting dark and milk chocolates. Use a Popsicle stick or toothpick to apply the contrasting chocolate to the inside of the mould during Step 2, before you clamp the mould halves together. Melt and pour the primary chocolate color as usual.

❅ ❅ ❅ CHOCOLATE SANTAS ❅ ❅ ❅
31

HARD CANDY SUCKERS

MATERIALS AND TOOLS

assorted antique or reproduction Santa lollipop moulds

lollipop sticks

2 cups granulated sugar

⅔ cup light corn syrup

⅔ cup water

few grains salt

two or three drops food coloring

¼ teaspoon flavoring oil

olive oil in a spray bottle

saucepan

candy thermometer

stove

spoons

baking sheet

DIRECTIONS

1. Wash the moulds with warm, soapy water and dry thoroughly. Spray the inside of each mould with olive oil. Set the moulds wrong side up on a flat baking sheet.
2. Combine sugar, corn syrup, water, and salt in a saucepan. Set over moderate heat, stirring constantly until mixture begins to boil.

3. Stop stirring and continue heating to 290°F (143°C) ("very brittle" stage on candy thermometer). Use a very low flame towards the end to prevent discoloration.
4. Add coloring and flavoring, stirring just enough to blend thoroughly.

5. Pour or spoon hot mixture into prepared moulds. Insert sticks about one-third of the way into each sucker while syrup is still hot. Give each stick a slight twist to secure it in the sucker.
6. Loosen the suckers from the moulds when they are firm but before they are completely cooled.

PERFECT HARD CANDIES

Follow these suggestions for clear candy suckers that stay hard and do not crystallize:

❄ Work on a clear, sunny, dry day. Avoid rainy days or hot, humid weather.
❄ Never stir once the sugar crystals are dissolved. Wipe off any crystals that form on the sides of the pan with a clean damp dishcloth.
❄ Wrap suckers in cellophane or wax paper. Store in a tightly covered tin or glass jar in a cool, dry place.

BEESWAX SANTA CANDLES

Beeswax is an excellent medium for bringing out the details of antique chocolate moulds. Pure, honey-toned beeswax is a natural product available from beekeepers.

It can be used as is or combined with other waxes for a lighter color. Either way, you will enjoy its spicy, pungent scent. The finished figures can be highlighted

with acrylic paints, and a light finishing coat adds a shine. The candles shown are 5", 7", and 9" tall.

❋ ❋ ❋ ❋

MATERIALS AND TOOLS

2 lbs. pure beeswax (makes three candles, as shown)

candlewicking

antique or reproduction metal chocolate Santa mould(s), two-piece with clamps

olive oil in a spray bottle

acrylic paints and paintbrush (optional)

water-based shiny finish (optional)

soft brush

coffee can

pot of water

measuring cup

stove

pliers

nail

knife

oven mitts

wide-mouthed container, 1″ taller than mould

clean dishcloths or paper towels

reusable putty adhesive

pencil

DIRECTIONS

1. Roll a piece of reusable putty adhesive into a long, skinny "sausage." Lay it on the inside flange of one mould half, close to the impression. Press the mould halves together to create a seal. Fill the mould with water; then pour out the water into the coffee can. Add ⅛ cup water for a small mould, ¼ cup water for a large mould. Scratch the water level onto the inside of the can with a nail as your "melting mark."

2. Pour out the water, and dry the can thoroughly. Use the pliers to bend the rim into a pouring spout.

TO PREPARE THE MOULD:

3. Pry the mould apart, and remove the putty. Wash both halves of the mould with warm, soapy water, rinse well, and dry thoroughly. Spray the inside of both halves lightly with olive oil.

4. Cut a piece of candlewicking 3″ longer than the height of the mould. Clamp the mould halves together over the wicking so that 1″ of wick protrudes from the top.

5. Turn the mould upside down, and nestle it vertically inside a wide-mouthed container cushioned with clean dishcloths or paper towels.

6. Set a pencil across the rim of the container. Wrap the free end of the wicking around the pencil, and secure with putty to hold the wicking straight and taut.

TO MELT THE BEESWAX:

7. Bring a pot of water to simmering and set the coffee can inside. Cut small chunks of beeswax with a knife, and set them in the can to melt. Keep adding beeswax in small amounts until the liquid wax reaches slightly above the melting mark. Carefully pour the hot liquid wax into the mould, filling it to the rim. In a few moments, the cooling wax will form a depression. Pour the remaining wax in the depression to fill it. Allow the candle to cool in the mould overnight.

Note: Throughout Step 7, do not leave stove unattended. Wear oven mitts when handling the hot can.

FINISHING:

8. Trim off the wicking close to the base. Unclamp the mould, and carefully remove the figure. Details on finished figures can be highlighted with acrylic paints. For a shiny surface, brush with water-based finish, working slowly to prevent air bubbles from forming. To make beeswax figures that are not candles, simply omit Steps 4 and 6.

RUSSIAN ST. NICHOLAS

The legendary St. Nicholas, the fourth-century bishop of Myra in Asia Minor, has been revered throughout Christendom for more than 1,500 years. According to popular lore, this kindly bishop saved an impoverished family from ruin by secretly dropping coins down its chimney at night. The coins fell into stockings hung by the fire to dry, providing dowries for the three marriageable daughters. The St. Nicholas figure shown here is modelled after an early twentieth-century decoration. Bracing the winter snows in an all-white coat, he offers a different look from the red-suited Santas usually seen. The coat is fashioned from cotton batting and wool roving, and the face is painted chalkware. The vine-entwined staff was discovered on a walk in the woods. The figure stands about 15" tall.

❄ ❄ ❄ ❄ ❄

MATERIALS AND TOOLS

painted chalkware Santa face, 2″ across, with two 16″ tie-on strings (see page 29)

½ yard 44″ prequilted cotton fabric

15″ × 21″ unbleached cotton batting

7″ × 14″ medium-weight polyester batting

4″ × 12″ off-white wool fabric

4¼″ × 6½″ red fabric

3½ yards white wool roving

fiberfill

dark green pearl cotton

7″ × 7″ of ¼″ plywood (for base)

two 18″ stems of 18-gauge florist's wire

12″ twig

white sparkling glitter

acrylic modelling paste

thick white tacky glue

clear arts-and-crafts glue

hot-glue gun

3½″ doll-making needle

stiff brush (for modelling paste and glue)

fabric marking pencil

staple gun

wire cutters

quilter's stencil plastic

DIRECTIONS

TO MAKE THE BODY:

1. Trace the actual-size body pattern. Cut two bodies from the prequilted fabric. To prevent stretching, stitch all curves ⅜″ from the edges.

2. Sew the two bodies together, leaving the straight bottom edge open. Clip the curves; then turn right side out. Make ½″ clips in the bottom straight edge every 1½″ (see pattern). Stuff firmly with fiberfill.

TO MAKE THE ARMS:

3. Cut a 7″ × 14″ rectangle from the remaining prequilted fabric. Lay the 7″ × 14″ polyester batting on top. Place the two 18″ florist's wire stems along one long edge so that the wires extend 2″ at each end. Roll up the batting and fabric tightly around the stems. Trim away the excess batting; then secure the long fabric edge with hot glue or by hand-sewing. Bend each wire extension into a small loop.

4. Cut the off-white wool fabric in half crosswise for two 4″ × 6″ pieces. Trace the actual-size mitten pattern onto stencil plastic and cut out. Using the mitten template and a marking pencil, mark two mittens (reverse one) on the wrong side of one fabric piece. Place both fabric pieces together, right sides facing, and sew through both layers along the curved lines only. Cut out the mittens ¼″ beyond the stitching. Clip the curves and turn right side out. Stuff fiberfill into each mitten.

Hand-stitch along the thumb line with off-white thread.

5. Slip the mittens onto the wire loops at each end of the arm piece. Hand-gather the batting around the mittens at wrists.

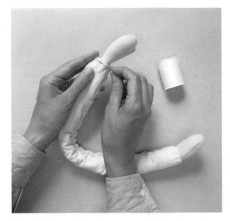

Padded wool mittens are joined to the stuffed arm piece (Step 5).

TO MAKE THE COAT SLEEVE:

6. Cut a 5½″ × 15″ piece of unbleached cotton batting. Sew the long edges together, making a ¼″ seam. Gently turn right side out. Carefully slide the arm piece through this sleeve. Hand-gather the ends of the sleeve around each mitten and sew in place.

7. Hand-sew the arm piece to the body back just below the neck. Reinforce with hot glue.

TO ATTACH THE FACE:

8. Thread each face string, in turn, through the doll-making needle, and draw the needle through the body diagonally, emerging at the small Xs. Make

sure the face is on the front of the body and the arms are on the back. Tie the strings together in pairs diagonally across the back of the head.

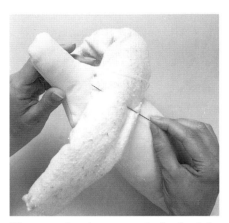

The arm piece is sewn to the back of the soft quilted-fabric body (Step 7).

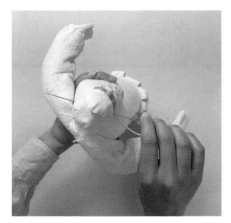

Two face strings are carried diagonally through the head portion using a long doll-making needle. The ends are tied together in back (Step 8).

TO MOUNT THE BODY ON THE STAND:

9. Stand the body upright on the plywood base. Arrange the lower edge in a circle by fanning out the clipped edge, and staple it to the

plywood. Fill out the skirt with additional fiberfill, if necessary, as you complete the stapling.

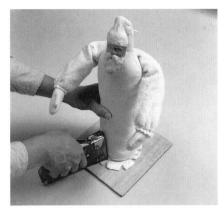

The lower edge of the body is clipped so that it fans out on the plywood base. A staple gun anchors the edge in place (Step 9).

10. Cut 1 yard of roving (set aside the rest for coat trim). Pad roving into any open areas around the face. Brush back of head with tacky glue and affix roving. Fill out the body by wrapping roving around the shoulders, torso, and upper arms.
11. Brush the exposed areas of the base with modelling paste; let dry, then coat again.

TO MAKE THE COAT:

12. Cut a 13″ × 14″ piece of unbleached cotton batting. Mark and cut two 2½″ armhole slits (Diagram 1).
13. Wrap the coat around the Santa body so that the arms correspond to the armhole slits. Fold the armhole edges to the inside; then bring the coat up and over the arm piece in the back and up and under the chalkware beard in the front. Tack the front and

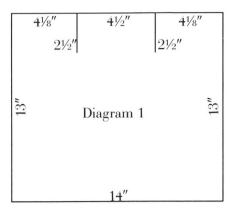

back together at the shoulders. Whipstitch the front edges together—they should just meet over the extra padding you added in Step 10. Stuff extra fiberfill around the chest and neck to fill out the hollows. Trim away any excess coat batting at the bottom edge.

The edges of the coat armhole slits are turned under before hand-sewing (Step 13).

14. Use a hot-glue gun to attach the reserved roving "fur" to the coat. Test-fit each length of roving on your St. Nicholas before you cut it. First, wrap the head with a circle of roving for a hat. Wrap a larger circle around the bottom coat edge, concealing the stapled tabs. Next,

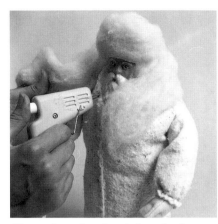

Natural wool roving is hot-glued around the neck of the coat, forming a deep shawl collar (Step 14).

wrap a piece up over the right front, around the back of the neck and head, and down the middle front to create a shawl collar effect. Finish by wrapping cuffs around the wrists, concealing the sleeve/hand join.

FINISHING AND TRIMS:

15. Brush clear glue sparingly on the base. Sprinkle the entire figure and the base lightly with glitter—the glitter will stick to the fibres in the roving without glue.

16. Fold the red fabric in half, right side in and shorter edges matching. Sew the shorter edges together to make a tube. Lay the tube flat with the seam at the middle, and sew one end closed. Turn the sack right side out and stuff with fiberfill. Gather the sack ¾″ from the top, and tie it closed with green pearl cotton. Tie the sack to St. Nicholas's left wrist.

17. Hot-glue the staff to the right mitten and to the base.

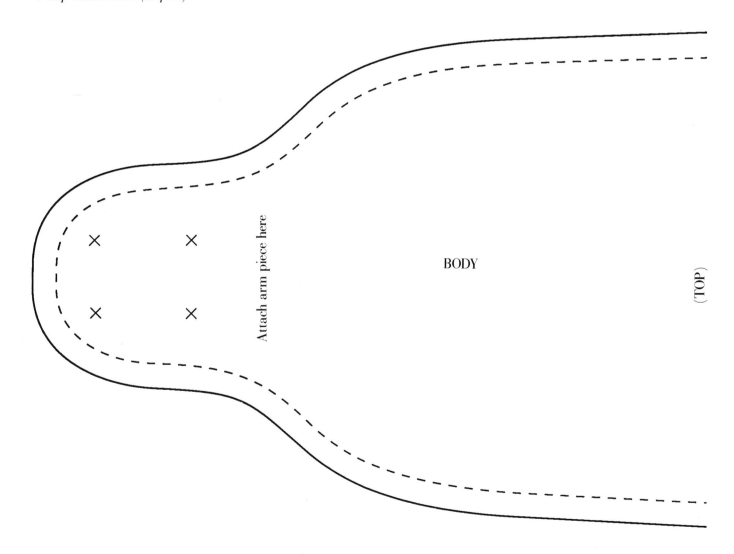

Attach arm piece here

BODY

(TOP)

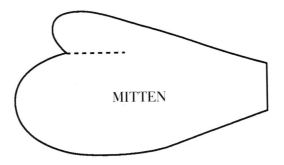

MITTEN

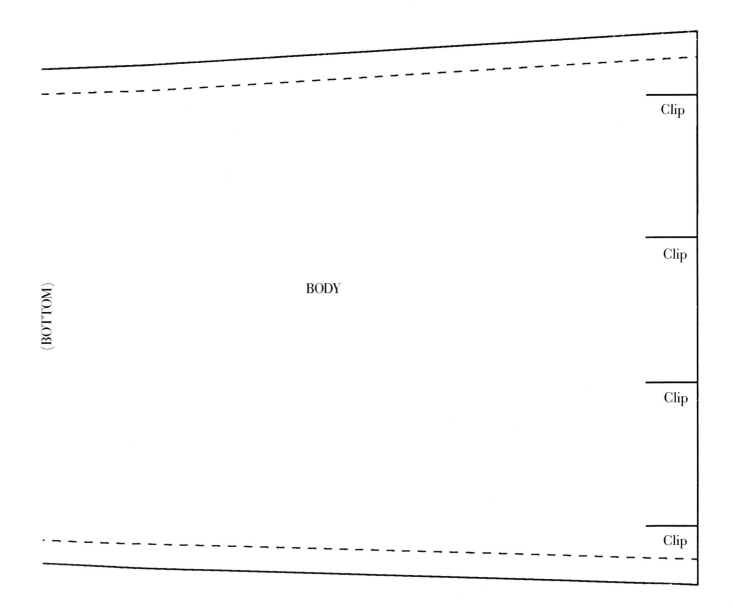

(BOTTOM)

BODY

Clip

Clip

Clip

Clip

VICTORIAN PINECONE SANTA

Instructions for this rustic Santa originally appeared in the December 1868 issue of Godey's Lady's Book. *Cones, moss, and a white flaxen beard contribute a "back-to-nature" aura, which was widely popularized in the Victorian age. The original instructions called for a papier-mâché face and hands, but this contemporary version substitutes sculpted balsa wood for papier-mâché. The wood of the American balsa tree is strong yet extremely lightweight. Beginning woodcarvers will find it easy to cut and shape, and they have the added assurance that "mistakes" will only add to the character of the piece. The figure stands about 19" tall.*

✳ ✳ ✳ ✳ ✳

MATERIALS AND TOOLS

four 5½" to 6½" Norwegian spruce cones, fully opened

1" × 1" × 12" balsa wood

3" × 3" × 3" balsa wood

5½" × 5½" × ⅝" pine (for base)

9" Styrofoam cone (3⅞"-diameter base)

10" white flax roving

7" × 13" nubby or plush brown fabric

fiberfill

2 oz. sphagnum moss

four 12" 20-mm pine chenille stems

four 18" stems of 18-gauge florist's wire

28-gauge steel wire

36" strand of miniature ornaments

assorted twigs and branches, up to 1¼" diameter

five small pinecones, about ½" across

red berry pips

two to three dozen plastic apples or berries, about ½" across

brown florist's tape

small mesh bag

two 2" No. 6 wood screws

hemp twine

black, blue, dark green, Caucasian skin tone, rose, and white acrylic paints

water-based antique finish

water-based matte finish

thick white tacky glue

medium and fine paintbrushes

stiff brush (for glue)

transparent ruler

craft knife with wood-carving blades

drill with 7/16", ⅛", and 1/16" bits

needle-nose pliers with built-in wire cutter

Phillips screwdriver

coping saw

vise

DIRECTIONS

1. Trace boots, hand, and face patterns.

TO CARVE THE BOOTS:

2. Tape boots tracing to 12" balsa wood. Go over traced lines with pencil, pressing firmly to leave indentation in wood. Remove tracing and cut out two A and two B pieces with a coping saw. Set aside excess balsa wood for hands.
3. Glue As to Bs at diagonal cuts to form two L-shaped boots (Diagram 1). When glue is thoroughly dry, use a craft knife to taper the toes and round all except the sole edges.

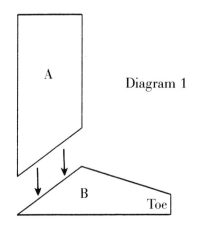

Diagram 1

TO CARVE THE HANDS:

4. Tape the hand tracing to reserved balsa wood, and go over traced lines as for boots. Lift the tracing, turn it over, and mark a second hand in the same way. You should have one right hand and one left hand.
5. Carve hands with a craft knife. Cut holes clear through fists, as marked. Gently shape edges. Score three lines on outer curved portion of hand to suggest fingers.

Holes are carved clear through the fists so that the finished figure can carry a feather tree and bird cage (Step 5).

TO CARVE THE HEAD:

6. Place the transparent ruler along the grain of the 3" balsa cube, and mark a parallel line ¾" in from one edge. Saw through the cube on line and discard excess. Turn the block, mark a second line along the grain, and saw off for a finished block size of 2¼" × 2¼" × 3".
7. Mark a dot at middle of 2¼" × 2¼" block base. Secure the block in a vise for drilling. Using a 1/16" bit, drill a hole 1½" deep at marked dot.
8. Tape the face tracing to one 2¼" × 3" side of block; it should fit

exactly and the wood grain should run from forehead to chin, with drilled hole at bottom. Go over all marked lines except eyes to indent wood. Remove tracing.

9. Using a craft knife fitted with a wood-carving blade, cut away the excess wood at forehead and chin, following face outline. Next, carefully scrape away the toned areas on pattern, leaving the eyebrows, nose, cheeks, and mouth in relief. You do not need to shape back of head.

10. Cut a 4″ length of 18-gauge florist's wire stem. Fill drilled hole with glue, insert wire, and let dry.

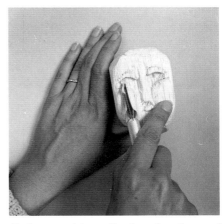

Balsa wood is easily shaved and carved away to shape the face details (Step 9).

TO PAINT THE FACE:

11. Paint the face Caucasian skin tone. Paint mouth rose. Paint eyebrows white. Referring to face pattern, paint a white almond-shaped eye under each eyebrow. Paint a round blue iris inside each eye. Paint a black dot pupil inside each iris. With a fine brush, paint a thin black line along the top arc of each white almond for eyelid.

Visualizing the iris as a clock face, paint a white dot highlight in each iris at the 1 o'clock position.

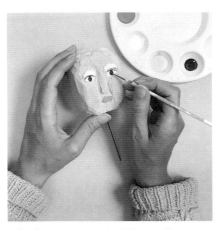

The face is painted with acrylics following the sculpted impressions and the pattern outlines (Step 11).

TO ASSEMBLE THE ARMS AND LEGS

12. Select one pair of similarly sized spruce cones for arms and one pair for legs; the legs can be a bit longer than the arms. Pick out some of the petals at the point of each cone to form a hollow. Test-fit hands and boots in each hollow; you may need to taper the wrists and boot tops with the craft knife to ensure a snug fit. Label all the pieces so that you can match them correctly later.

13. Paint the hands Caucasian skin tone. Using a fine brush, apply brown paint to the score lines between the fingers. Paint the boots black. Let dry.

14. Apply tacky glue generously to each hollow, and insert appropriate carved piece; hold until glue is set.

Before you test-fit the boot in the bottom of the pinecone, remove some of the petals (Step 12).

Choose cones that are comparable in size for arms and legs. Cones that curve slightly will add a realistic lilt to the finished Santa.

TO MAKE THE BODY:

15. Saw 2″ off the top of the Styrofoam cone. Trace the actual-size hip socket cutting guide. Tape the tracing to the base of the cone. Go over the traced lines with a pencil to leave an impression in the Styrofoam. Remove the tracing.

16. With a craft knife, carve two leg sockets in the base of the cone, using the marked indents as a guide. As you sculpt, test-fit the spruce cone legs in the sockets until the fit is snug.

17. Hold legs and Styrofoam body in position on the 5½″ × 5½″ × ⅝″ pine base. Have a partner trace the boots outline on the base with a pencil. Remove legs and body, and set aside. Mark a small dot within the heel section of each boot outline. Drill through the base at each dot using a ⅛″ bit.

18. Paint the base dark green. Let dry. Brush the boots, hands, face, and base with antiquing finish (test first in an inconspicuous place, and dilute finish with water if necessary). Let dry thoroughly.

19. Cut two 9″ lengths of 18-gauge florist's wire stem. Wrap one stem end around the "hip" section of a cone leg so that the wire sinks in between the petal layers. Pull tight to secure; then bend extension straight up. Repeat for second leg. Place the legs (but not the Styrofoam body) back in position on the base. Drive screws into the underside of the base, through the drilled holes and up into the balsawood boots. The screw should pass through boot section A and lodge firmly in section B.

20. Apply glue generously to the hip sockets on the Styrofoam body and to the top of each cone leg. Push the body down onto the leg wires, guiding it so that the wire stems lodge inside the Styrofoam and the hip sockets rest snugly on the legs. Wrap 28-gauge wire around the entire Styrofoam/pinecone hip section to further secure the legs. The wire will slip in between the petals and should not be visible.

Florist's wire and glue help keep the lightweight Styrofoam body securely attached to the legs (Step 20).

21. Cut two 12″ lengths of 18-gauge florist's wire stem. Wrap stem ends around upper arms, as for legs, bending extensions straight out to sides perpendicular to cones. Insert the extensions into the Styrofoam body at each side, about 1″ from top, so that arms fall at sides. Wrap the excess around the entire Styrofoam/pinecone shoulder area, slipping it in between the petals to hold the cone arms tight. Reinforce the join with tacky glue.

Florist's wire stems are allowed to sink in between the pinecone petals for a firm yet invisible join (Step 21).

TO ATTACH THE HEAD:

22. Apply glue generously to base of head and flat top section of Styrofoam body. Position the head above the body, and gently push down so that the head wire lodges inside the Styrofoam. Hold until glue is set.

TO MAKE THE HOOD:

23. Trace the actual-size hood pattern. Cut out one hood from brown fabric, remembering to place pattern on fold. Fold hood in half, right sides facing, and sew back seam. Turn to right side.

24. Brush glue on sides and top of head. Position hood on head and hold until glue is set. Push fiberfill up into hood at back of head to fill it out.

TO ADD THE MOSS:

25. Cut the remaining florist's wire stems into 2″ lengths. Bend each one into a hairpin shape to make florist's pins. Brush a small section of the Styrofoam body with glue. Press moss in place over glue, and secure with a pin. Repeat until entire body is covered and moss drapes down over top of legs like a tunic.

26. Brush glue around edge of hood, including back. Press small clumps of moss into glue for hood trim. Glue small pinecones and red berry pips to front.

Glue and florist's pins secure small clumps of sphagnum moss over the entire body (Step 25).

TO MAKE THE BEARD:

27. Unfurl flax roving. Reserve two small hanks for moustache and hair. Fold remaining roving in half, and glue folded section to chin under mouth. Glue moustache hank between nose and mouth. Tuck remainder under hood above forehead.

TO MAKE THE FEATHER TREE:

28. Cut three pine stems into thirds, for nine 4″ sprigs. Hold the remaining 12″ stem so that the needles point up. Beginning at the bottom, wrap this long stem tightly with florist's tape; unwind the tape directly from the roll, and stretch it as you wrap.

29. When 3″ of the stem is wrapped, place the bottom end of a 4″ sprig (make sure needles point up) against the long stem. Wrap the tape over the end of the sprig to secure it to the base stem. Add a second short sprig, then a third short sprig, making a complete

wrap after each one. Bend the three sprigs away from the main stem.

30. Carry the tape up over the nearest sprig, and continue wrapping the main stem for 2″. Add three more sprigs, one by one, as before. Repeat this step one more time to add a third tier of branches. Then wrap the tape back down the stem, stopping ½″ from the end. Cut the tape and end off.

31. Twist a red pip to the tip of each branch. Starting at the top, drape the strand of miniature ornaments from branch to branch. Insert stem of feather tree into Santa's right hand, and secure with glue.

TO MAKE THE BIRD CAGE:

32. Select a branch approximately 1¼″ in diameter. Secure the branch in a vise for drilling. Using a ⁷⁄₁₆″ bit, drill a hole clear through the branch. Saw off the excess branch ½″ below the hole. To make pitched roof, make two 45° diagonal cuts that meet in a point about ¾″ above the hole.

33. Select a stick about ⅜″ in diameter, and cut three 2¾″ lengths. Saw each length in half at a 45° angle. You should have six pieces, each with one slanted end and one straight end.

34. Cut a 20″ length of hemp twine. Fold in half and knot to form a 1″ loop. Glue loop to roof pitch with knot at top. Conceal loop by gluing six "logs" on top, three on each side, so angled cuts meet at the top. Tie ends of rope to Santa's left wrist. Insert small bundle of sticks into his left hand.

TO ATTACH THE SACK:

35. Fill the mesh sack with plastic apples. Tie sack closed at top. Secure to moss with a florist's pin, concealing it under beard.

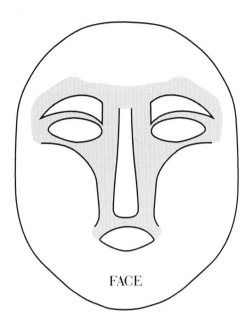

FACE

HAND

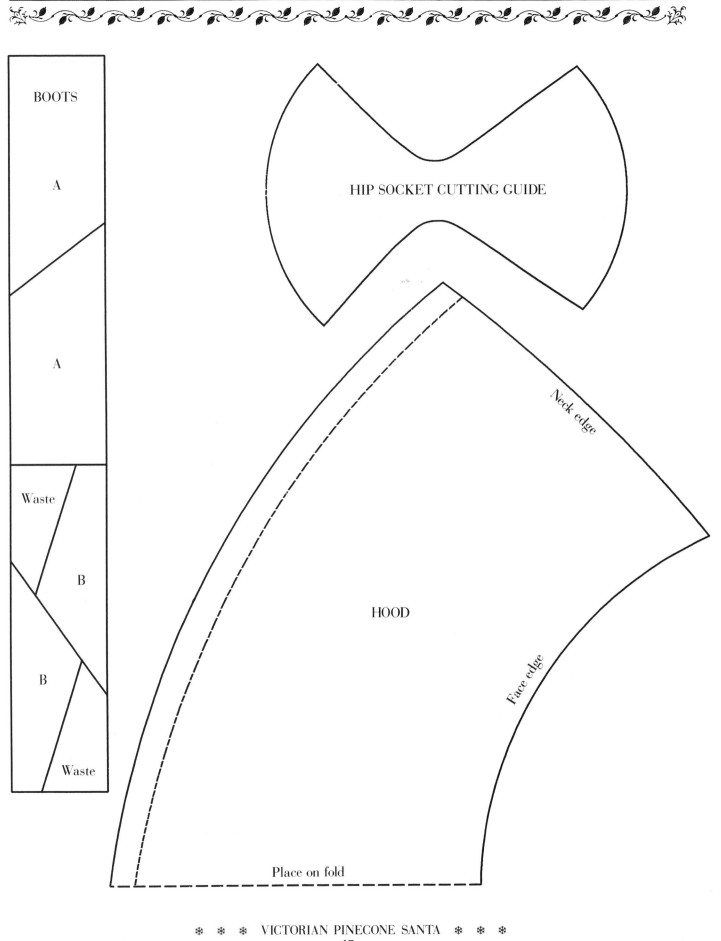

BOOTS

A

A

Waste

B

B

Waste

HIP SOCKET CUTTING GUIDE

HOOD

Neck edge

Face edge

Place on fold

PART
Two

COLLECTIBLE ORNAMENTS

❄ ❄ ❄ ❄ ❄ ❄ ❄ ❄

In the mid-1800s, an exciting, new printing technology—chromolithography, or color printing—transformed publishing and advertising. Printing had been developing since the 1500s, but color pigments had always been painstakingly applied to illustrations and borders by hand. The new chromolithography technology used the press itself to apply the color. Up to twenty colors could be applied in succession, with drying time in between. The process was fast, accurate, and so economical that merchants could afford to distribute complimentary bookmarks, trade cards, fans, calendars, and other printed paper novelties to promote their products.

In addition to advertising cards, printers found a ready consumer market for color postcards, greeting cards, and small die-cut pictures called "scraps." Available at stationery and department stores, scraps were sold in sheets and could be cut apart to use individually. They were purchased by men, women,

and children in every station of life. People fashioned scraps into ornaments, enclosed them in letters, and amassed impressive collections in scrapbooks.

Santa Claus was a popular subject for Victorian era scraps and greeting cards. In the growing and diverse American society, Santa offered a comfortable secular handle on the Christmas holiday that people of different Christian denominations could enjoy. Popular images downplayed his saintly roots, and showed instead the kindly "jolly old elf" depicted by Clement C. Moore in A Visit from St. Nicholas. *Picture postcards of Santa loaded down with toys, making dolls in his workshop, or riding in his reindeer-drawn sleigh fired children's imaginations. Santa wasn't all nostalgia and fantasy though. He joined right in on the exciting march into the twentieth century, by talking on the telephone, delivering presents by motorcar, even flying in on zeppelins and airplanes!*

Images of Santa, children, and angels turn up again

and again in Christmas ornaments made from the mid-1800s through the 1930s. Before 1870, when F. W. Woolworth introduced German glass-blown ornaments in his five-and-ten-cent stores, most ornaments were made at home from paper. Scraps could be used in many ways. A simple cutout trimmed with tinsel-wrapped wire resulted in a glittery, swirling ornament to hang on the tree. Some scraps were printed double in a mirror image. The picture folded over on itself and tinsel, garland, or spun glass bird tails were sandwiched between, for a hanging ornament that could be viewed from either side.

Another popular paper ornament was the cone-shaped cornucopia. The cone was rolled from paper, sometimes several layers, and decorated with tinsel, scraps, and bits of lace and ribbon. The prettiest ones were covered in shiny paper and used contrasting colors inside and out. Children loved them, for they dangled from the low tree branches, brimming with nutmeats, sweets, raisins, and candied citrus peel. Family and visitors helped themselves to these tempting delicacies throughout the twelve days of Christmas, and children eagerly awaited the Epiphany ritual of taking down the tree, because they were allowed to pick off the last remaining treats hidden among the branches.

Cotton batting, the commonplace filler for thousands of household quilts, also found its way into nineteenth-century ornaments. Magazines offered flat patterns for Santas, angels, stars, and other motifs  that could be copied onto cardboard or stiff paper. The batting was cut to shape and glued to the cardboard. Details and outlines were highlighted with tinsel, glitter, crepe paper, and buttons, an at-home project children relished. Often, a realistic scrap face would top a comparatively crude body, giving these ornaments a naïve charm all their own.

In Germany, beginning around 1890, the making of three-dimensional batting ornaments developed into a lucrative cottage industry. The white fibres were moistened with a glue mixture and wrapped around a wire or cardboard form to create figures, fruits, and vegetables. The glue-treated batting dried to a firm, semihard shell, for ornaments that were lightweight and unbreakable—perfect for families with young children who longed to touch and handle the trinkets of Christmas.

By the turn of the twentieth century, the typical household's Christmas tree featured a hodgepodge of colors and materials. Handmade and store-bought ornaments were mixed together with abandon. Families often splurged on one or two glass kugels, or blown-glass balls, for their ornament collection each year, while continuing to make ornaments at home using batting, scraps, crepe paper, glitter, and assorted trims.

The ornaments featured in this section include pieces that were traditionally made in the home as well as those produced by hand in cottage industries and small factories well into the twentieth century.

TINSEL AND SCRAPS

Here is a small collection of ornaments made with glittery tinsel and printed scrap pictures. Each one is in the spirit of late nineteenth-century ornament making, when a bit of this and a bit of that, combined with a pretty picture, could set children's minds racing to the holiday ahead. The easy-to-follow directions are sure to inspire your own creations.

❋ ❋ ❋ ❋ ❋

SANTA AND GIRL

Bendable tinsel wire creates a soft halo around Santa and his young friend. You can use this idea to accent a purchased scrap picture or a figure cut from a Christmas card.

MATERIALS AND TOOLS

scrap picture on heavy cardboard, 5″ to 10″ tall

silver or gold metallic tinsel wire on roll

silver icicles

medium-weight cardboard

scrap of paper

thick white tacky glue

stiff brush (for glue)

stapler

wire cutters

DIRECTIONS

1. Cut a cardboard rectangle slightly smaller than the scrap picture. Extreme precision is not necessary, but do make sure picture conceals the rectangle completely.
2. Unroll about 2 feet of tinsel wire, but do not cut. Bend an 8″ section of wire into a loop, crossing the wire over itself. Hold the loop behind the picture, adjust the size larger or smaller as desired, and then staple the loop to the cardboard rectangle at the crossover. Do not cut wire.
3. Bend an adjacent section of wire into a second loop. Hold the picture over the cardboard, adjust size and position of loop, and staple at crossover. Continue shaping wire into continuous free-form loops until entire picture is surrounded; end with an odd number of loops.
4. Set cardboard on a flat surface, tinsel side up, and brush generously with glue. Lay icicles across glued area. Place scrap picture on top and hold until set.
5. Glue a scrap of paper to the back of the cardboard to conceal the staples. Trim ends of icicles to length desired.

SNOWFLAKE VIGNETTES

Each of these holiday scenes was recycled from a Christmas card and then mounted on a glitter-covered plastic snowflake. For best results, choose contrasting tinsel trim. The reverse side can be decorated too.

MATERIALS AND TOOLS

glittery plastic or cardboard snowflakes, about 4″ across

old Christmas cards

assorted tinsel-wire trims

thick white tacky glue

stiff brush (for glue)

compass

wire cutters

lightweight cardboard

DIRECTIONS

1. Measure the snowflake diameter. Set the compass for this measurement minus 1½″, and draft a circle on cardboard. Carefully cut out and discard the circle, leaving a window template.
2. Lay the window template on a Christmas card. Move the template over the surface of the card to frame different views. Outline the selected view with a pencil; then remove the template and cut out the picture.
3. Brush reverse side of picture with a thin coat of glue. Center it, glue side down, on a snowflake and press until set. Glue second picture to reverse side of snowflake if desired. Bend tinsel-wire trim to shape around picture(s), snip off excess, and glue in place.

SNOWFLAKE FANCIES

Shimmering gold icicles contrast against silver snowflakes in these light-catching ornaments. Each is trimmed with a cutout scrap.

MATERIALS AND TOOLS

silver glittery plastic or cardboard snowflakes, about 4″ across

purchased scraps or old Christmas cards

gold icicles

thick white tacky glue

stiff brush (for glue)

DIRECTIONS

1. Test-fit scrap or cutout on snowflake, and trim if necessary.
2. Brush snowflake with glue, and lay gold icicles across it, from side to side. Press in place.
3. Brush back of scrap with glue. Position on middle of snowflake, over icicles, and press in place. Trim ends of icicles to length desired.

SPUN GLASS SKIRTS

Fan-shaped "bird tails" made of spun glass were a favorite trim in Germany's cottage ornament industry. Spun glass was initially developed for industrial use, but in the town of Lauscha, it was used exclusively for ornament making. The individual spun glass fibres were secured at one end with strong glue. They were used as skirts for Santa and angel paper ornaments and later as tail feathers for blown-glass birds. For more ornaments featuring spun glass, turn to pages 56 and 98.

MATERIALS AND TOOLS

3″ or 4″ spun glass bird tails

Santa and angel scraps, up to 2½″ across

foil medallions or wreaths, up to 2¾″ across

1¾″ dimensional foil starburst

lightweight cardboard

thick white tacky glue

hot-glue gun

stiff brush (for glue)

DIRECTIONS

TO MAKE SANTA:

1. Trim off Santa's coat below the waist. To reinforce paper scraps, mount on lightweight cardboard and cut out.
2. Turn Santa wrong side up. Apply hot glue to waist area. Press end of bird tail into glue. Fan out slightly and hold until set. You can use this method with any Santa or angel, including Santa faces.

TO MAKE ANGELS:

3. Apply hot glue to wrong side of foil medallion or wreath. Apply bird tail, and fan out as in Step 2 above. Turn to right side. Using tacky glue, affix foil trims and angel scraps as desired.

TINSEL SANTAS

Two glittery ornaments combine tiny chalkware faces and gold tinsel stems. Both are easy to craft and can be used to trim gift packages as well as the Christmas tree.

The lyre Santa would make a fitting memento for someone with musical interests. Santa Starburst is 5½" across; Santa on a Lyre is 4½" × 5½".

❊ ❊ ❊ ❊ ❊

SANTA STARBURST

MATERIALS AND TOOLS

painted chalkware Santa face, ⅞″ across (see page 29)

five 12″ 6-mm gold tinsel stems

12″ 6-mm white chenille stem

small piece red wool fabric

white wool roving

evergreen sprig with pips

medium-weight cardboard

thick white tacky glue

stiff brush (for glue)

compass

needle-nose pliers with built-in wire cutter

string

sheet of typing paper

wax paper

DIRECTIONS

TO MAKE THE STARBURST:

1. Using a compass, draft a 5¾″- diameter circle on typing paper. Reinsert the compass point into the same hole, and draft 4½″- and 1½″-diameter concentric circles. Next, draft a 1½″-diameter circle on cardboard. Cut out the cardboard circle only.

2. Cut three 12″ tinsel stems in half, for six 6″ lengths. Cut the two remaining stems in thirds, for six 4″ lengths.

3. Bend each tinsel stem into a hairpin loop; hold the ends together, and twist once with pliers to secure. You should have six long loops and six short loops.

4. Brush a generous amount of glue onto the cardboard circle. Position the cardboard circle, glue side up, on the typing paper template. Arrange the loops evenly around it, alternating long and short. Press the twisted end of each long loop into the glue so that each loop touches the outer circle on the template. Fill the spaces in between with short loops, using the middle circle as a guide. Lay a sheet of wax paper on top, and weight with a heavy book overnight or until dry.

TO MAKE THE HAT:

5. Wrap a string once around the chalkware head at hat line to determine measurement A. From red fabric, cut a rectangle (A + ¼″) × 2″. Fold in half, right side in and 2″ edges matching. Sew diagonally from corner to corner. Trim away loose excess and turn to right side.

FINISHING AND TRIMS:

6. Place hat on Santa head with seam at back. Bend white chenille stem to shape around the hat edge and trim off excess. Glue in place, concealing raw edge. Twist remaining chenille stem around a pin three times to form a pom-pom; trim off excess. Glue pom-pom to tip of hat.

7. Glue Santa head to starburst, covering tinsel-loop ends. Glue a small tuft of roving to chin for beard.

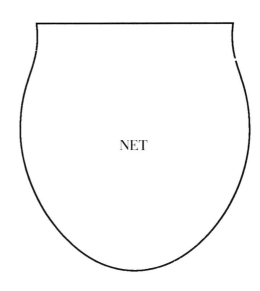

NET

SANTA ON A LYRE

MATERIALS AND TOOLS

painted chalkware Santa face, ⅞″ across (see page 29)

12″ 6-mm gold tinsel stem

12-mm gold loop tinsel wire on roll

small piece gold netting

small piece red wool fabric

white wool roving

thick white tacky glue

stiff brush (for glue)

black felt-tip pen

wire cutters

DIRECTIONS

1. Unroll about 2 feet of gold loop tinsel wire, but do not cut. Place the wire on the actual-size lyre pattern, and bend it into the lyre shape. Trim away the excess.

2. Cut a 3½″ length of 6-mm gold tinsel stem. Place it across the front of the lyre; then bend the ends to the back at dots. Secure with tacky glue.

3. Bend the remaining tinsel stem in half to form an inverted **V**. Bend each end up 1¼″. Overlap these ends and glue them together, forming a long, narrow triangle. Glue the lapped section across the back of the lyre between dots to create a hanger.

4. Trace the actual-size net pattern. Go over the marked lines

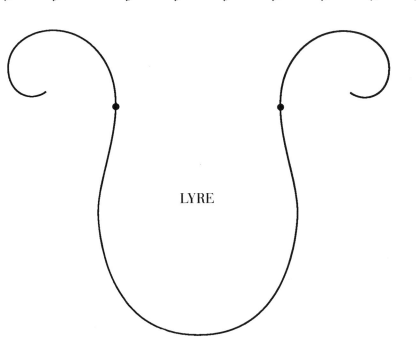

LYRE

with a black felt-tip pen. Lay the gold netting on top of the tracing and tape down. Following the pattern lines visible through the netting, cut out the netting only. Glue to wrong side of lyre.

TO MAKE THE HAT:

5. Same as Santa Starburst, Step 5.

FINISHING AND TRIMS:

6. Place hat on Santa head with seam at back. Pull out a hank of roving about ⅜″ in diameter. Roll the fibres in your fingers to compress them. Glue around hat edge, and trim away excess. Roll a pea-sized ball of roving, and glue to tip of hat for pom-pom.

7. Glue Santa head to front of lyre between dots. Glue a small tuft of roving to chin for beard.

SANTA ON A SWING

The German cottage ornament industry was the first to turn out this snappy Santa on a swing. The flexible pipe cleaner body is covered with crinkled paper, and a scrap face adds a touch of realism. To hang this ornament, simply slip the wide arch onto a Christmas tree branch with plenty of clearance. A gentle nudge will set the swing in motion. The ornament is about 7" high.

MATERIALS AND TOOLS

Santa scrap face, ½" to ¾" across

14" red paper twist

two 12" black pipe cleaners

18" stem of 18-gauge florist's wire

12" 20-mm pine chenille stem

28-gauge steel wire

black pearl cotton, size 3

gold garland scrap

two red berry pips

ice-cream stick

brown shoe polish

thick white tacky glue

stiff brush (for glue)

needle-nose pliers with built-in wire cutter

awl

soft cloth

DIRECTIONS TO MAKE THE SWING:

1. Use a soft cloth to rub shoe polish on ice-cream stick. Let "stain" seep in for a few minutes; then wipe off excess.

2. Mark a small dot ⅜" from each end of the ice-cream stick. Pierce through each dot with an awl. You can repair minor splits with glue.

3. Trim green florist's wire stem to 17". Cut three 24" lengths of 28-gauge steel wire. Hold the three steel wires together. Wrap them around the florist's wire in a tight spiral from end to end. Insert all four wire ends through an ice-cream stick hole and bend them into a small kink on the underside. Repeat on the opposite hole to make the arched hanger.

4. Cut two 4" lengths from pine stem. Wrap a pip wire around each stem so that berry is at top. Beginning at ice-cream stick platform, twist pine stems tightly around each side of swing wire for about 2½". The spiraled steel wires will prevent the pine stems from slipping.

TO MAKE SANTA:

5. Cut paper twist into one 7", one 3", and eight ½" lengths. Carefully unfurl all pieces.

6. Cut one 11" and one 5½" stem from black pipe cleaners. Brush each stem with glue; then wind the ½" paper twist strips around them, spiral fashion, until completely covered. Let dry.

7. Bend the 11" covered stem in half to form an inverted V. Make

L-shaped bends ½" from each end to form feet. Hold this piece vertically with the feet at the bottom. Place the shorter covered stem across it about ½" from the top, forming a lowercase T shape. Glue in position and let dry.

8. Fold the unfurled 7" paper twist piece in half so that ridges run perpendicular to the fold. Place this tunic over the torso with the fold at the top, and glue at the T crossover.

9. Cut a 6" length of black pearl cotton. Tie an overhand knot at each end; then fluff out the ends to make tassels. Wrap around tunic for a belt, drawing in at the waist, and tie in front. Shape shoulders and

skirt with your fingers. Glue scrap face to upper torso. Crumple a scrap of gold garland, and glue between face and belt for button.

10. Cut a 1¾" × 3" rectangle from remaining paper twist. Lay the rectangle on template A, and make folds 1–3 as indicated. Lay the folded piece on template B, and complete folds 4 and 5, for finished hat C. Fit the hat around head, covering top of scrap face. Overlap points in back and glue.

FINISHING:

11. Stand Santa on swing. Bend hands over swing wire, and glue in place. Glue feet to platform.

HAT TEMPLATES

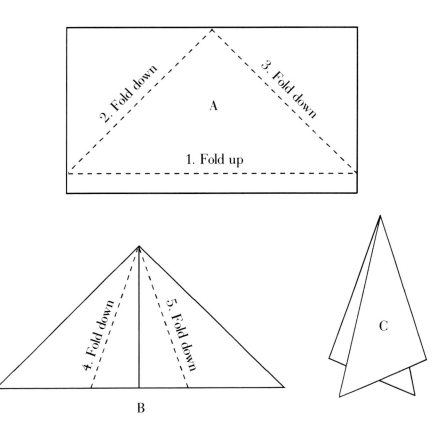

ANGEL ON A CLOUD

*This heavenly angel lithograph
floats in a cloud of spun glass
fairies' hair. The radiant "beams
of light" are actually individual
bird tails grouped close together.
For an especially dazzling effect,
suspend this ornament in front of
a mirror or anywhere it can catch
the light. It is about 8" across.*

❊ ❊ ❊ ❊ ❊

MATERIALS AND TOOLS

angel scrap face with wings on heavy cardboard, about 4″ across

three 4″ spun glass bird tails

pale green curly fairies' hair

two 1¾″ gold plastic starbursts

"Merry Christmas" baker's or florist's pick, about 3½″ long (break off stick)

4½ × 4½″ ultra-thin cotton batting or recycled Christmas tree drape

medium-weight cardboard

thick white tacky glue

hot-glue gun

stiff brush (for tacky glue)

compass

DIRECTIONS

TO MAKE THE BACKING:

1. Use a compass to draft a 3¾″-diameter circle on cardboard. Reinsert the compass point into the same hole, and draft a ¾″-diameter concentric circle. Cut on the larger circle line.

2. Brush the unmarked side of the cardboard circle lightly with tacky glue. Place the circle, glue side down, on the batting, and press until the glue is set. Trim the batting ⅜″ beyond the circle outline. Clip into this allowance every 1″ all around. Brush glue around the edge of the cardboard circle, fold the allowance onto it, and press firmly until set.

TO ATTACH THE BIRD TAILS:

3. Arrange three spun glass bird tails evenly around the lower half of the circular backing so that the compact glued ends touch the inner circle and the tails extend 2½″ beyond the outer edge. Fan out the tails so that they touch each other at the sides. Hot-glue in place, one by one.

FINISHING AND TRIMS:

4. Position the angel face above the bird tails, concealing the top of the circle. Brush cardboard area underneath angel with tacky glue. Press angel in place and hold until glue is set.

5. Arrange pale green fairies' hair around the angel face, concealing cardboard and glued ends of bird tails. Glue in place.

6. Brush tacky glue on the back of the plastic starbursts and the "Merry Christmas" pick. Position on bird tails and hold until set. You can remove any stray glue from the bird tails with a damp cloth.

BASIC CORNUCOPIAS

The basic "pointed-top" cornu-copia is rolled from a square of holiday giftwrap. You can choose matching or contrasting giftwrap for the liner. Before printed papers were available, homemakers rolled Christmas cornucopias from plain white or brown paper and pasted scraps on the outside. We suggest using scrap paper for your first two or three tries until you get the knack of rolling a sharp point. The cones are about 8½" long.

❄ ❄ ❄ ❄ ❄

MATERIALS AND TOOLS

assorted Christmas giftwraps

crochet thread

clear arts-and-crafts glue

stiff brush (for glue)

mechanical pencil

transparent ruler

craft knife

awl

self-healing cutting mat

Diagram 1

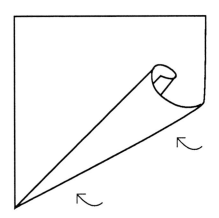

Diagram 2

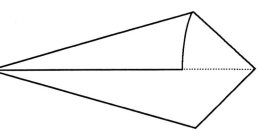

Diagram 3

DIRECTIONS

1. Place the giftwrap on a cutting mat, wrong side up. Using a transparent ruler and a craft knife, cut one 6" square (outside) and one 6¼" square (lining).

TO ROLL THE CORNUCOPIA:

2. Place the 6" square on flat surface, wrong side up. Bend the lower right corner up about ½" and make an angled crease ending in a sharp point at the lower left corner (Diagram 1).

3. Place your left thumb on the paper just above the point. With your right hand, begin rolling the folded edge up to create a tight cone shape. Keep your left thumb in position to direct the bottom of the cone into a sharp point. Don't worry about the size of the cone during this step (Diagram 2).

4. As you complete the rolling, insert the thumb of your right hand inside the cone. Lift the cone with your left hand, and turn it so that the loose flap and the point at the right are on top. Slowly let the cone "relax" until the straight edge of the flap aligns with the point. Use the fingers of your right hand to hold the cone at this shape throughout Step 5 (Diagram 3).

5. Lay the cone back down on a flat surface, let the flap unfurl, and brush glue along the inside flap edge. Lift the cone once more, and press the flap back against it; hold until glue is set. Turn so that the flap is in back.

TO MAKE THE LINER:

6. Lay the 6¼″ square on a flat surface, right side up. Following Steps 2–5 above, make a second cone. The printed surface will appear on the inside.

FINISHING:

7. Slip the liner inside the outer cone. Position both pieces so that the top edges are parallel and the liner extends about ⅜″ above the outer cone. With scissors, clip into this extension at the front **V** until you reach the outer cone edge. Make two more clips, evenly spaced, on

each side of the **V**, for a total of five clips all around.

8. Brush glue around the top edge of the outer cone just below the liner extension. Fold the extension down, one section at a time, over the glued area and hold until set. Brush on extra glue at the top point to secure the multiple layers.

TO ATTACH THE HANGING CORD:

9. Use an awl to pierce a small hole in the top point through all layers. Cut a 5″ length of crochet thread. Insert both ends into the hole, and tie in an overhand knot in back.

DOUBLE-CORNUCOPIAS

Make two cones with liners following Steps 1–8 for Basic Cornucopias. Slip one cone inside the other. Turn the cones so that the top points are opposite and the sides slope towards each other, forming two **V**s. With an awl, pierce a small hole about ⅜″ below the point of each **V** through all layers. Cut a 9″ length of crochet thread. Insert each end into a hole, and knot on the inside for a hanging cord.

FANCY
CORNUCOPIAS

Yesteryear's confectionery shops sold holiday sweets in cornucopias that could be hung on the Christmas tree. The crepe paper tops folded down to protect the candies packaged inside. You can re-create the Victorian look using holiday and wedding giftwraps, metallic trims, cutouts, and stickers. The cones are 6" to 8" long, including the crepe paper tops. The same design also looks lovely without the tops.

❋ ❋ ❋ ❋ ❋

MATERIALS AND TOOLS

white-on-white wedding giftwrap, Christmas giftwrap featuring Victorian Santas, or other giftwrap of your choice

assorted metallic trims, including lace, cord, paper edgings, and tinsel

holiday stickers

crepe paper (streamer or sheet)

metallic yarn

metallic crochet thread

white artist's matte tape

clear arts-and-crafts glue

stiff brush (for glue)

compass

transparent ruler

DIRECTIONS

1. Place giftwrap right side up on a flat surface. Using a compass, draft an 11"-diameter circle. Align transparent ruler on central hole, and draw a line dividing the circle in half. Cut out on marked lines. Each half-circle makes one cornucopia.
Note: Refer to Diagram 1 for placement of image on pictorial giftwrap. The area marked by the **X** *will appear on the front of the cone.*

TO ROLL THE CORNUCOPIA:

2. Place one half-circle on a flat surface, wrong side up and with straight edge at left. Bring the lower section up to the top, matching the corners and edges; do not crease. Rotate the top layer to the right about ⅝". Make sure curved edges are matching; then press down and crease firmly (Diagram 2).
3. For a deep top, cut a piece of crepe paper 4" × 9" with the vertical ridges parallel to the 4" edge. For a short top, cut a 9" crepe paper streamer. Apply a bead of glue along the curved edge of the folded cone paper. Position the 9" crepe paper edge on top. Glue the ends first, keeping edges aligned; then work towards middle. The extension will "pop up" as you round the curve (Diagram 3).
4. Place your left thumb on the left edge of the cone paper just above the crease. With your right hand, begin rolling the folded edge up to create a tight cone shape. Keep your left thumb in position to direct the bottom of the cone into a sharp

point. Don't worry about the size of the cone during this step (Diagram 4).
5. As you complete the rolling, insert the thumb of your right hand inside the cone. Lift the cone with your left hand, and turn it so that the loose flap is on top. Slowly let the cone "relax" until the straight edge of the flap overlaps the folded edge by about 1" at the top. Use the fingers of your right hand to hold the cone at this shape throughout Step 6.
6. Same as Basic Cornucopias, Step 5 (page 60).

TO ATTACH THE HANGING CORD:

7. Use a sharp needle to pierce a hole in each side of the cone about ⅜" below the rim. Cut a 12" length of metallic yarn. Insert each end into a hole, and secure with white matte tape on the inside.

FINISHING AND TRIMS:

8. Cut an 8½" length of gold or silver trim. Apply a bead of glue around the top edge of the paper cone. Press the trim onto the glue, overlapping the ends at the back. Affix a sticker or cutout picture to front of each plain cone.
9. After you fill the cornucopias, gather the deep crepe paper tops with your fingers and have a partner tie on metallic crochet thread.

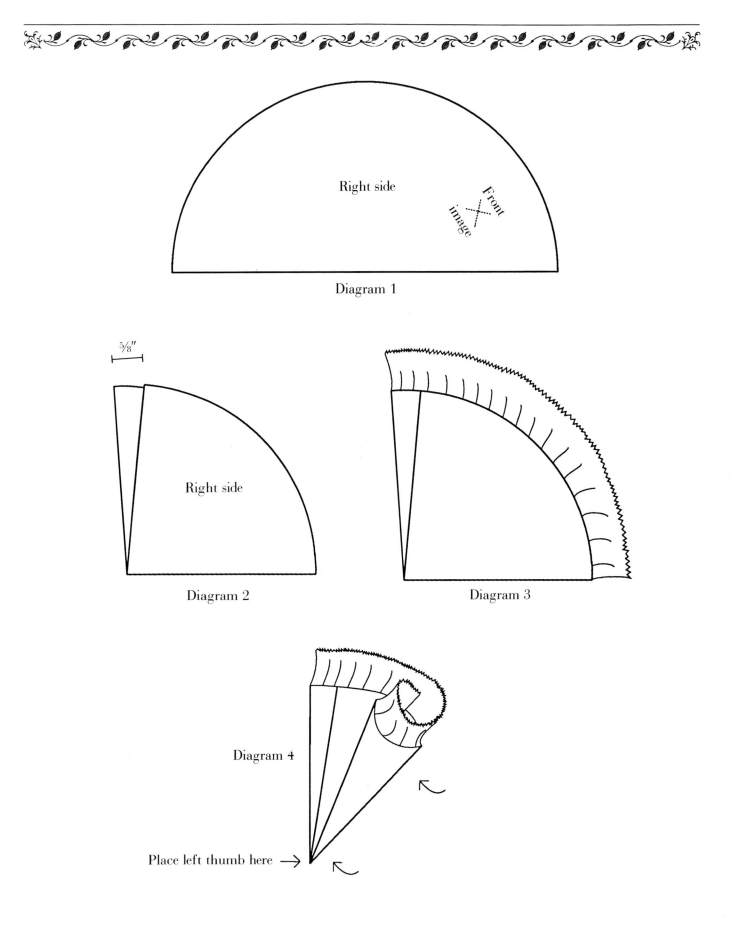

Right side

Front
image

Diagram 1

5/8″

Right side

Diagram 2

Diagram 3

Diagram 4

Place left thumb here →

BEADED STARS

These simple, light-catching ornaments are made of glass beads, pearls, and sequins strung on wire. During the Victorian era, women's magazines gave instructions for stringing bead ornaments at home. These same projects offer today's crafters the opportunity to recycle old costume jewelry, Christmas garland beads, and sewing trims. Try one or two stars following the directions; then experiment with different designs using beads from your own collection. Dimensions will vary, depending on the bead size used.

❋ ❋ ❋ ❋ ❋

LARGE STAR WITH SHAMROCK

MATERIALS AND TOOLS

75 15-mm glass garland beads, assorted colors

approximately 160 5-mm green sequins

approximately 160 green rocaille beads

21-gauge florist's wire

34-gauge beading wire

needle-nose pliers with built-in wire cutters

DIRECTIONS

TO MAKE THE STAR:

1. Cut a 60″ length of 21-gauge florist's wire. Make a kink 4″ from one end. Beginning at the other end, string on 40 glass garland beads. Strive to vary the colors, but for the best effect, use the same color for beads #1, #16, and #31, which will be star points. Push the beads all the way down to the kink (Diagram 1).

2. Lay the strand on a flat work surface with the kink at the top. Carefully shape two rounded star "points" at beads #16 and #31. Then, with bead #40 positioned between beads #6 and #7, wrap the free wire around the strung wire once (Diagram 2).

3. String on 11 more beads, making the sixth bead in the point color. Bend this new section at the sixth bead to shape the third point. Wrap the free wire around the strung wire four beads from first wrap (Diagram 3).

4. Add four more beads and wrap the wire five beads from the nearest point (Diagram 4).

5. Repeat Steps 3 and 4 one more time. Add the remaining five beads. Carefully unbend the kink, and complete the point by passing the wire end through bead #1 (Diagram 5).

6. Use pliers to twist the two wire ends together. Bend this spiraled

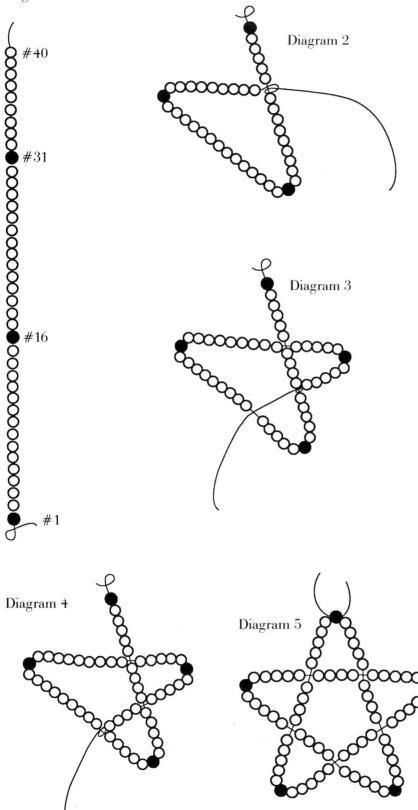

Diagram 1

#40

#31

#16

#1

Diagram 2

Diagram 3

Diagram 4

Diagram 5

section into a hanging loop; then wrap the base several times tightly to secure it. Cut off any excess wire.

TO MAKE THE SHAMROCK:

7. Sort sequins and rocaille beads into two separate saucers.

8. Cut a 16″ length of 34-gauge beading wire. Make a V-shaped bend 2″ from one end. Slip one rocaille bead onto the wire so that it rests in the crook of the bend. Next, slip two beads onto the wire at the long end. As you slide them down, hold the shorter end parallel so that the beads cover both wires (Diagram 6a).

9. Push all three beads as close together as you can make them; then twist the short wire around the long wire tightly several times. Cut off excess (Diagram 6b).

10. String on a sequin so that the "cup" faces down. Add a bead, then another sequin. Continue alternating beads and sequins for 5″. For easier stringing, do not pick up individual beads with your fingers—instead, try inserting the wire directly into the holes.

11. To create the top cloverleaf, bend the green stem into a curve and wrap the free wire around the stem 1½″ from the end. The beads and sequins should be snug but with enough give so that you can slip the wire between them for wrapping (Diagram 7).

12. Continue stringing beads and sequins for another 7″. Join the new section to the main stem by twisting the free wire over the previous wrap. You will have formed a large floppy loop (Diagram 8).

13. To create the two side cloverleafs, draw this large loop down in an eyeglass shape and wrap once more over the previous wraps. Cut off the excess wire.

14. To make a hanger, cut a 4″ length of wire. Bend it in half, and slip it around the top cloverleaf. Twist the wires together in a tight spiral; then bend into a hook shape. The shamrock can be hung from the large star or on its own.

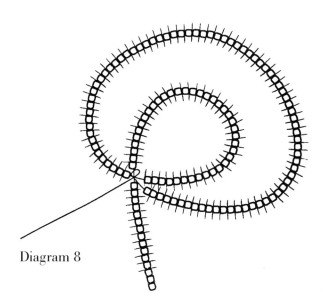

Diagram 8

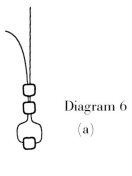

Diagram 6
(a)

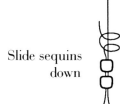

Slide sequins down

(b)

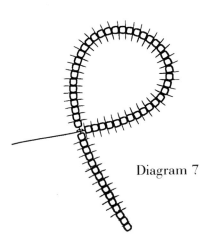

Diagram 7

SMALL STAR WITH FLOWER

MATERIALS AND TOOLS

70 6-mm green pearlized beads

5 6-mm blue glass beads

5 10-mm gold glass beads

60 3-mm white pearls

28-gauge steel wire

34-gauge beading wire

heavy-duty sewing thread

needle-nose pliers with built-in cutter

DIRECTIONS

TO MAKE THE STAR:

1–5. Cut a 30″ length of 28-gauge steel wire. Proceed as for the Large Star with Shamrock, Steps 1–5, using green pearlized beads for the star body and blue glass beads for the points.

6. Tie a gold glass bead inside each point. For each, cut an 8″ length of heavy-duty sewing thread. Wrap the middle of the thread once around the star wire two balls from the point. Slip both 4″ thread ends through a gold bead. Wrap each thread end individually, in reverse rotation, around the star wire opposite. Tie the ends together in a tight double-knot and cut off excess.

TO MAKE THE PEARL FLOWER:

7. Cut a 14″ length of 34-gauge beading wire. Make a kink 2″ from one end. Beginning at the other end, string on 17 pearls. Slide them all the way down to the kink.

8. To create a flower petal of 10 pearls, bend the strand into a curve and wrap the free wire between pearls #7 and #8 (Diagram 1).

9. String on 12 more pearls. Make a second petal of 10 pearls by wrapping the wire two pearls from the first wrap (Diagram 2).

10. Repeat Step 9 until four petals are made. Add two more pearls and wrap the wire two pearls from first wrap (Diagram 3).

11. Add the remaining five pearls. Using pliers, carefully unbend the kink and twist the two wire ends together. The finished flower can be tied onto the small star or hung on its own.

Diagram 3

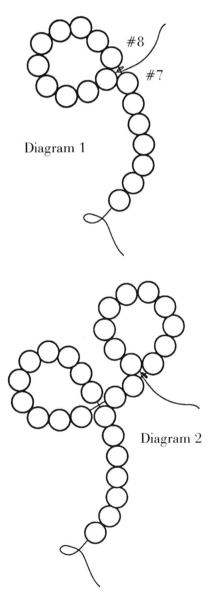

Diagram 1

Diagram 2

SMALL STAR WITH BALL

MATERIALS AND TOOLS

70 6-mm aqua glass beads

5 10-mm gold glass beads

small silver glass ball

28-gauge steel wire

heavy-duty sewing thread

needle-nose pliers with built-in wire cutter

DIRECTIONS

1–5. Cut a 30″ length of 28-gauge wire. Proceed as for the Large Star with Shamrock, Steps 1–5, using aqua glass beads for the star body and gold glass beads for the points.

6. Using heavy-duty thread, tie the silver glass ball between two aqua beads so that it hangs in middle of star.

BUGLE BEAD STAR

MATERIALS AND TOOLS

40 12-mm gold bugle beads

5 6-mm green pearlized beads

small red glass ball

28-gauge steel wire

heavy-duty sewing thread

needle-nose pliers with built-in wire cutter

DIRECTIONS

1. Cut a 30″ length of 28-gauge steel wire. Make a kink 4″ from one end. Beginning at the other end, string on one green bead (star point), eight bugle beads, one green bead (star point), eight bugle beads, one green bead (star point), and five bugle beads (Diagram 1).

2. Lay the strand on a flat work surface with the kink at the top. Carefully shape two star points at the second and third green beads. Then, with the last bugle bead positioned between the third and fourth bugle beads, wrap the free wire around the strung wire once (Diagram 2).

3. String on three bugle beads, one green bead, and three bugle beads. Shape the star point at the green bead. Wrap the free wire around the strung wire two bugle beads from first wrap (Diagram 3).

4. Add two more bugle beads, and wrap the wire three bugle beads from the nearest point (Diagram 4).

5. Repeat Steps 3 and 4 one more time; then add the remaining three bugle beads. Carefully unbend the kink, and complete the point by passing the wire end through the first green bead (Diagram 5).

6. Use pliers to twist the two wire ends together. Bend this spiraled section into a hanging loop; then wrap the base several times tightly to secure it. Cut off any excess wire.

7. Using heavy-duty thread, tie the red glass ball between two bugle beads so that it hangs in middle of star.

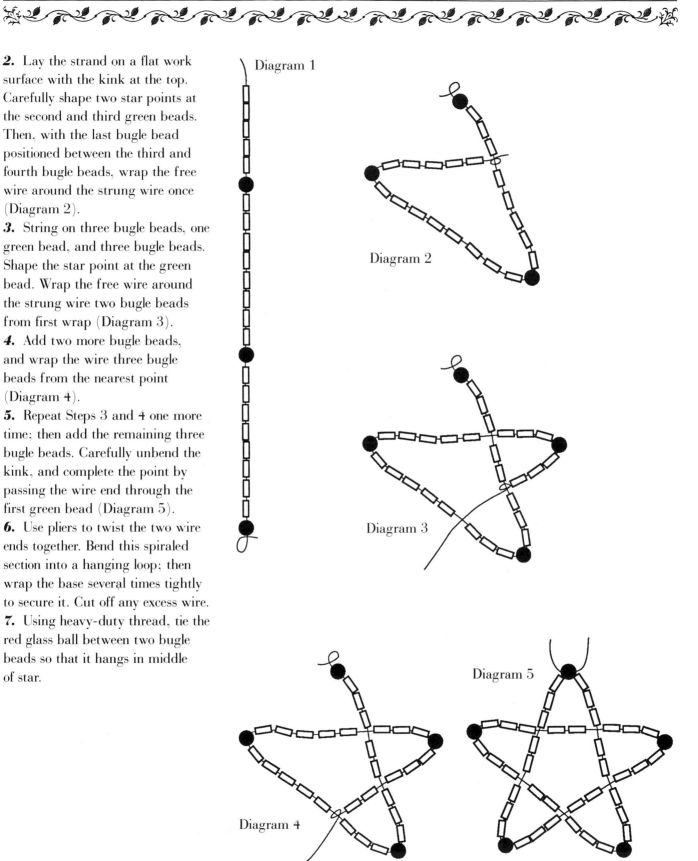

Diagram 1

Diagram 2

Diagram 3

Diagram 4

Diagram 5

VICTORIAN NET SANTAS

These doll-like Santas are actually small gift bags, perfect for holding candy, nuts, coins, or jewelry. Each one opens and closes at the back with a drawstring. Santa ornaments made of net first appeared during the late Victorian era, and Japanese manufacturers continued to produce them in the early twentieth century. To make them at home, you'll need to purchase the open-meshed fabric used for laundry sacks. The large Santa is 11" high, and the smaller version is 7½" high.

✳ ✳ ✳ ✳ ✳

BASIC MATERIALS AND TOOLS

acrylic modelling paste

black acrylic paint

thick white tacky glue

stiff brush (for modelling paste and glue)

mechanical pencil

black felt-tip pen

marking pencils (one dark, one light)

one sheet 11″ × 17″ graph paper (¼″ squares)

stencil plastic

tea-dyed roving (to tea-dye, see box on page 84)

fiberfill

red and green embroidery floss

LARGE NET SANTA

ADDITIONAL MATERIALS AND TOOLS

painted chalkware Santa face, 1¾″ across × 3″ long, with 16″ drawstring (see page 29)

12″ × 36″ coffee-dyed mesh or net (to coffee-dye, see box above)

2″ × 24″ muted green broadcloth

6″ × 6″ red wool fabric

12″ × 12″ pink flannel fabric

24″ ecru 1″ lace with burgundy ⅛″ ribbon insertion

three small red ball-type buttons

ANTIQUING WITH COFFEE

Use this easy dye method to antique synthetic as well as all-cotton mesh fabrics. To prepare the solution, dissolve ⅛ cup instant coffee in two cups boiling water. Dip the mesh in the hot solution, and soak until the desired darkness is achieved—usually for 1 to 5 minutes. Keep in mind that mesh will look slightly darker when wet. A clear glass bowl will help you judge the color better. Lay on old, clean terry towels to dry.

DIRECTIONS

TO MAKE THE ARMS AND BOOTS:

1. Trace the actual-size arm and boot patterns onto stencil plastic, and cut out to make templates. Fold the pink flannel piece in half, right side in. Lay the templates on top, and trace around edges with a dark marking pencil. Repeat to mark two arms and two boots.

2. Machine-stitch on the curved lines only. Cut out ¼″ beyond marked lines, and turn right side out. Stuff the arms lightly with fiberfill. Stuff the boots solidly.

3. Brush the surface and top of the boots with modelling paste. The paste will seep into the fabric and fiberfill and dry to a semihard finish. When dry, paint boots black.

TO MAKE THE NET-BAG SUIT:

4. Referring to Diagrams 1 and 2, use a ruler and a mechanical pencil to draft suit A and sleeve B on graph paper. Go over the marked lines with a black felt-tip pen.

5. Fold the mesh in half crosswise. Lay doubled mesh on top of the graph paper pattern and tape down. Following the pattern lines visible through the mesh, cut out the mesh only. You should have two As and two Bs.

6. Fold each mesh A in half, matching the diagonal edges. Sew the diagonal edges together in a ¼″ seam to make legs. Turn one A right side out, and insert it into the other A with edges matching. Sew one continuous seam front to back.

7. Fold each mesh B in half crosswise. Sew 5″ edges together to make sleeve. Turn to right side.

8. Fold the wrist edge of each sleeve ¼″ to the wrong side and hand-baste in place. Insert an arm into the sleeve. Pull the basting thread to gather the wrist around the hand and tie off. Wrap the wrist with red embroidery floss to conceal the gathering thread.

9. Hand-gather sleeve top around upper arm, matching the top edges so that sleeve puffs out. Lay the suit face up on a flat surface, with front and back seams matching. Lay arm/sleeve pieces at sides so that top edge is 1″ below top edge of suit. Pin in place.

10. Fold the ankle edge of each suit leg ¼″ to the wrong side, and hand-baste in place. Draw basting threads tight around boot tops; tie off thread and secure with glue. Wrap with green embroidery floss.

TO ATTACH THE COLLAR:

11. Sew short edges of green fabric together and press seam open. Fold long edges ¼″ to wrong side and press. Hand-sew lace with ribbon insertion along one edge, beginning at seam.

12. Turn neck edge of net suit ⅝″ to wrong side and baste. To form casing, pin plain edge of collar to suit ¼″ from folded net edge, matching collar and back seams.

Topstitch through all layers along collar edge. Sew buttons to front below collar.

TO MAKE THE HAT:

13. Fold the red wool fabric in half diagonally, right side in. Trace the actual-size hat pattern onto stencil plastic. Cut out on marked lines to make a template. Lay the template on the wool triangle, and trace around edges with a light marking pencil. Machine-stitch on marked long edges; do not stitch short straight edges. Cut out ¼″ beyond marked lines. Turn to right side. Glue to chalkware head with seams at sides.

14. Pull out hank of tea-dyed roving about ⅜″ in diameter. Roll the fibres in your fingers to compress them. Glue around hat, concealing raw edge; trim away excess. Roll a pea-sized ball of roving, and glue to top of hat for pom-pom.

FINISHING:

15. Hold chalkware face at front of suit. Insert drawstring ends into neck casing at front seam. Draw the ends through the casing, one to each side, and pull out at back. Fill bag with candy; pull draw-strings tight and tie ends in a bow.

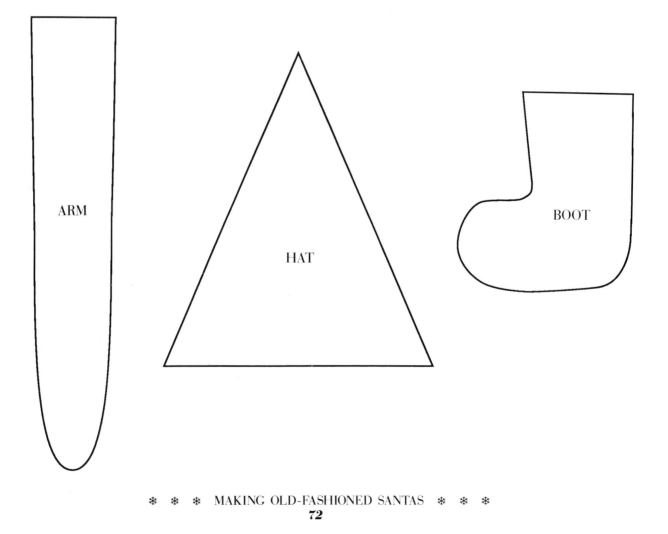

ARM

HAT

BOOT

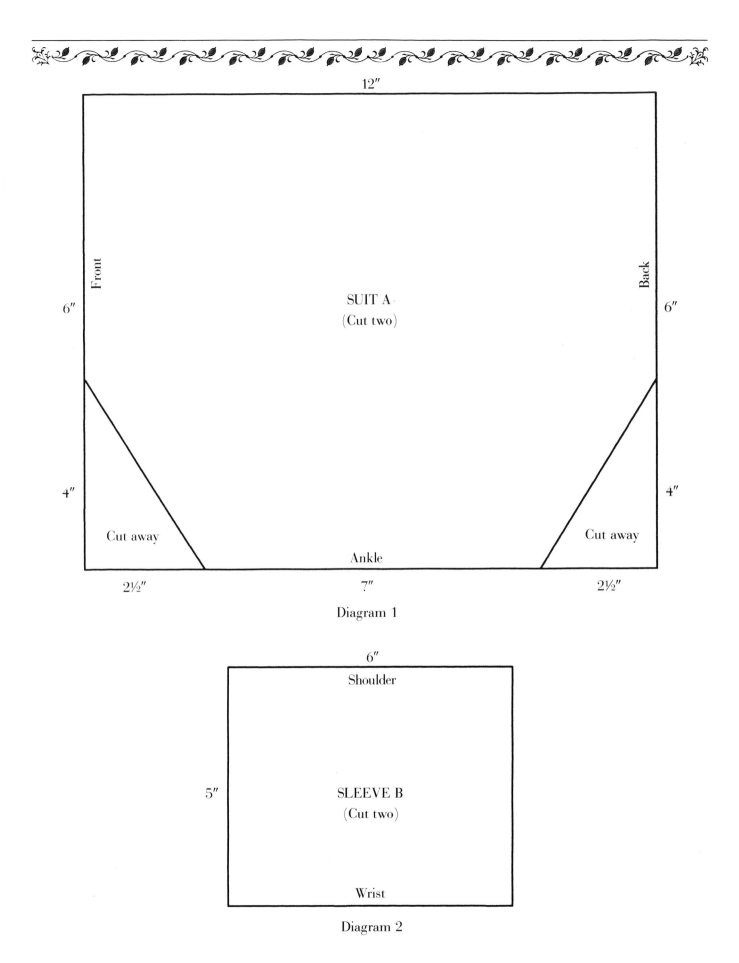

12"

Front

Back

6" 6"

SUIT A
(Cut two)

4" 4"

Cut away Cut away

Ankle

2½" 7" 2½"

Diagram 1

6"

Shoulder

5" SLEEVE B
(Cut two)

Wrist

Diagram 2

SMALL NET SANTA

ADDITIONAL MATERIALS AND TOOLS

painted chalkware Santa face, 1″ across × 2″ long, with 12″ drawstring (see page 29)

8″ × 24″ coffee-dyed mesh or net (to coffee-dye, see page 71)

12″ burgundy seam binding

5″ × 5″ red wool fabric

7″ × 7″ pink flannel fabric

12″ ecru ½″ lace with green ¹⁄₁₆″ ribbon insertion

three miniature jingle bells

DIRECTIONS

TO MAKE THE ARMS AND BOOTS:

1–3. Same as Large Net Santa, Steps 1–3.

TO MAKE THE NET-BAG SUIT:

4–10. Same as Large Net Santa, Steps 4–10, substituting AA and BB for A and B.

TO ATTACH THE COLLAR:

11. Sew short edges of burgundy seam binding together and press seam open. Hand-sew lace with ribbon insertion along one edge, beginning at seam.

12. Turn neck edge of net suit ⅝″ to wrong side and baste. To form casing, pin plain edge of collar to suit ¼″ from folded net edge,

matching collar and center back seams. Hand-sew through all layers along collar edge. Sew jingle bells to front below collar.

TO MAKE THE HAT:

13 and 14. Same as Large Net Santa, Steps 13 and 14.

FINISHING:

15. Same as Large Net Santa, Step 15.

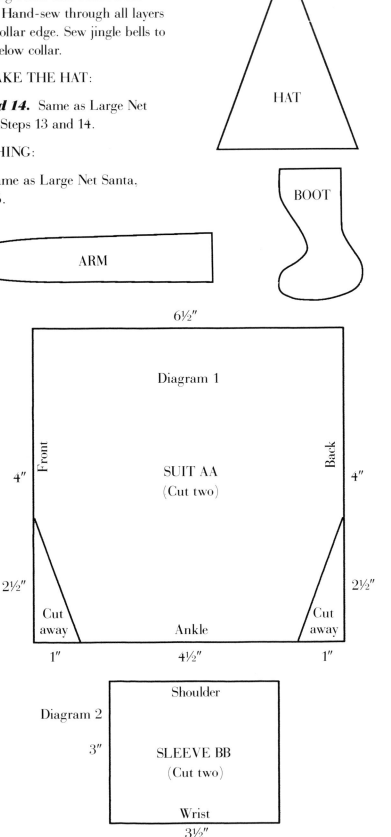

JAPANESE NET SANTAS

Net Santa ornaments originating in Japan were especially popular during the 1920s and 1930s. Factory-made, they were assembled from paper, wood, moulded composition, and artificial trims. Crafters can achieve the "early plastic" look by moulding faces and hands with modelling compound. The small pieces of net required for the three projects that follow can be cut from old net curtains, fishnet stockings, produce packaging, and mesh laundry bags. You're sure to run across additional sources that you can recycle.

❋ ❋ ❋ ❋

NET SANTA SLEIGH

These fanciful sleigh runners were cut from basswood with a jigsaw. If your woodworking tools or experience are limited, you can still achieve an authentic look with 5-ply posterboard. The use of wood was actually more typical on ornaments made in Germany; most Japanese manufacturers economized with heavy cardboard. This ornament is about 7½" long × 6" high.

MATERIALS AND TOOLS

painted modelling-compound Santa face, 1¼" across, with 24" drawstring (see box opposite)

two painted modelling-compound hands, ½" across × 1" long (see box opposite)

4" × 12½" coffee-dyed mesh or net (to coffee-dye, see box on page 71)

5" × 6" red fabric

⅜" × 15" strip ecru fake fur *or* two 12" 15-mm ecru chenille stems

4" × 16" × 3/16" basswood *or* 7" × 9" 5-ply white posterboard

3½" × 5½" × 3/16" balsa wood

½" × ½" × 4¼" balsa wood

batting

three miniature silver jingle bells

red acrylic paint

fabric stiffener

thick white tacky glue

glue applicator

paintbrush

stiff brush (for glue)

mechanical pencil

transparent ruler

fine sandpaper

tabletop jigsaw (optional; to cut basswood runners)

vise

coping saw

craft knife

DIRECTIONS

1. Measure and mark balsa-wood rectangle for one 2½" × 3½" floor and six ½" × 3½" slats. Mark ½" × ½" × 4¼" balsa-wood strip for two 2⅛" braces. Cut all pieces with a coping saw.

2. Make two tracings of actual-size runner pattern. Tape both tracings to basswood or posterboard.

BASSWOOD ONLY:

3. Retrace the marked lines with a pencil, pressing firmly to leave an indentation in wood. Remove tracing paper. Go over all indented lines with a pencil to highlight them. Cut out using a tabletop jigsaw. *Wear protective goggles and follow the manufacturer's directions.* When you are finished, sand all edges. Skip to Step 5.

POSTERBOARD ONLY:

4. Using a transparent ruler and a craft knife, carefully score all straight lines, pressing the knife through the tracing paper and into the posterboard. To score curving lines, hold the knife steady and rotate the posterboard away from you. Remove the tracing paper, and score again to deepen the cuts. Cut out both runners with sharp scissors.

5. Cut a 3¾" × 4¾" piece of red fabric. Lay it on a flat surface, wrong side up, and set balsa-wood floor on top. Brush the floor edges with glue. Fold the excess fabric onto the floor edges, corners first, and hold until set.

6. Paint runners and remaining wood pieces with red acrylic paint. Let dry.

TO MAKE THE SLEIGH BASE:

7. Stand two of the ½" × 3½" slats on edge and parallel for sleigh sides. Using the glue applicator, apply glue generously to both ends of each brace. Set the braces between the sides ¼" from the ends. Hold until glue is set (Diagram 1).

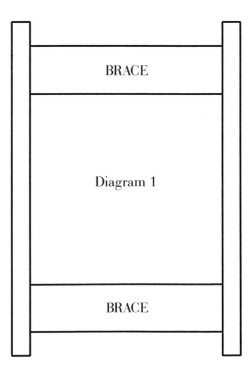

BRACE

Diagram 1

BRACE

5. Apply a bead of glue to top of sides and braces. Lay the remaining four slats on top so that the outer slats are even with sides and spacing between slats is even (about ⅛″). The slats will extend ¼″ beyond the braces at each end. Hold until glue is set (Diagram 2).

TO ATTACH THE RUNNERS:

9. Lay the runners wrong side up on a flat surface. Run a thick bead of glue along each side of the sleigh base. Referring to the pattern for position, press a gluey edge onto the top section of one runner. Let set a few minutes. Lift the piece carefully, and join to the other runner. Set the entire assembly upside down in a vise. Make any final adjustments; then continue to hold the runners in position while a partner tightens the vise. Remove from vise when dry.

TO ATTACH THE NET BAG:

10. Fold mesh in half, shorter edges matching. Sew shorter edges together to make a tube.
11. Fold one edge of tube ½″ to the wrong side. Stitch ⅜″ from folded edge to form casing. Turn right side out.
12. Apply a bead of glue to top of slats along outer edges only. Turn raw edge of net bag under ½″ and press into glue; make sure bag seam is at back of sled. Apply glue around edge of floor on wrong side. Insert floor inside bag, glue side down, on top of slats, concealing bag edges. Hold until glue is set.

Diagram 2

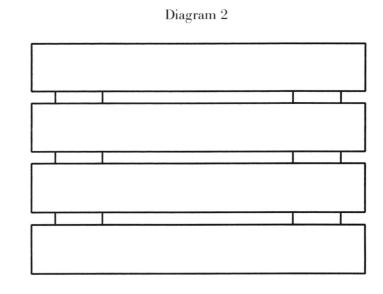

"MOULDED PLASTIC" HEADS AND HANDS

If you've made the chalkware heads on page 29, you'll find the modelling-compound version very easy. Work a ball of modelling compound in your fingers for a few minutes to soften it; then press it into the face area of the chocolate mould. Be sure to pick up the full beard impression. Make the back flat and even with the mould edges. Lay the cord or drawstring across the back, and mould a separate piece of modelling compound over it to anchor it in place. To remove the face, gently loosen the edges and pull it from the mould without stretching it.

For each hand, roll a pea-sized ball of modelling compound into a sausage; then flatten it slightly to the length and width desired.

Bake all the pieces immediately in a 275°F (135°C) oven for 20 minutes, or as suggested on the modelling compound package instructions. Let cool completely. Then add acrylic colors, antiquing, and matte finish; see Chalkware Belsnickels, Steps 6, 8, and 9 (page 28), for detailed instructions.

TO MAKE THE HAT:

13. Same as Santa Starburst, Step 5 (page 52).

14. Glue hat to top of head. Section off a hank of roving fibres about ⅜″ in diameter. Roll the fibres in your fingers to compress them. Glue around hat, concealing raw edge; trim away excess.

TO ATTACH THE HEAD AND ARMS:

15. Locate front of net bag. Insert drawstring ends into casing at this point. Draw the ends through the casing, one to each side, and pull out at back seam. Head will appear at front of bag.

16. Cut two 1¾″ × 2″ sleeves from red fabric. Fold each piece in half, right side in and shorter edges matching. Sew shorter edges together to make a tube. Turn right side out. Stuff lightly with fiberfill.

17. Brush glue on the wrist section of each hand. Slip wrist into open end of sleeve, and hold until glue is set. Roll more roving trim and glue around wrist, concealing raw edges.

18. Sew upper end of each sleeve shut. Tack to casing edge of net bag behind head.

FINISHING:

19. Brush mesh with a light coat of fabric stiffener. Let dry.

20. Cut a 2″ piece from fake fur strip. Glue down front of net bag under beard. Glue remaining fake fur around base of net bag, trimming off excess. Thick chenille or roving can be used instead of fake fur.

21. Sew two jingle bells to fur at front. Sew remaining jingle bell to top of hat. Glue decoration of your choice to front of hat.

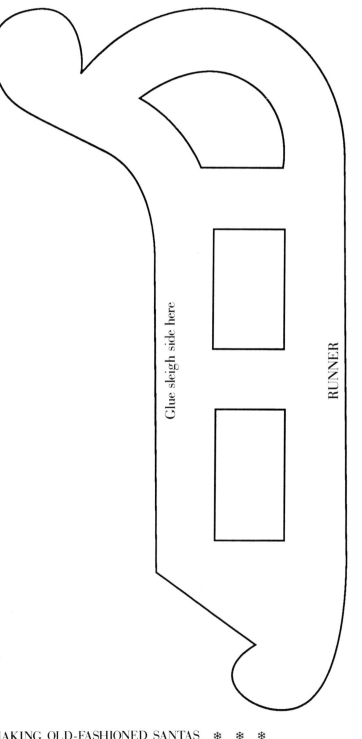

Glue sleigh side here

RUNNER

NET SANTA BASKET

Any small wicker or wooden basket would make a good base for this net Santa ornament. You can also use a cane basket, although the paint won't adhere as well. This ornament is about 5″ high.

MATERIALS AND TOOLS

painted modelling-compound Santa face, 1″ across, with 24″ drawstring (see box on page 77)

two painted modelling-compound hands, ⅜″ across × ¾″ long (see box on page 77)

coffee-dyed mesh or net (for size, see Step 2 below; to coffee-dye, see box on page 71)

6″ × 6″ red velour fabric

small natural basket, about 3″ across

two 12″ 6-mm white chenille stems

fabric stiffener

red acrylic paint

thick white tacky glue

glue applicator

paintbrush

stiff brush (for glue)

DIRECTIONS

1. Break or cut handle off basket. Paint basket with red acrylic paint. Let dry.

TO ATTACH THE NET BAG:

2. Measure the basket opening perimeter and add ½″. Cut a mesh rectangle this length × 3½″.

3 and 4. Same as Net Santa Sleigh, Steps 10 and 11 (page 77).

5. Apply a bead of glue to outside edge of basket opening. Turn raw edge of net bag under ½″. With seam at the back, press folded edge into the glue and hold until set. Bend a chenille stem to shape around basket and trim off excess. Glue in place around basket edge, concealing join.

TO MAKE THE HAT:

6. Same as Santa Starburst, Step 5 (page 52).

7. Lay hat flat with seam centered at back. Thread a needle with matching sewing thread and knot the end. Place the needle inside the hat, and draw it out at the tip, lodging the knot inside. Sew tiny ⅛″ running stitches along right edge of hat for ½″. Pull to gather the hat into a curve. Tie off thread ends securely.

8. Same as Santa Starburst, Step 6 (page 52).

TO ATTACH THE HEAD AND ARMS:

9. Same as Net Santa Sleigh, Step 15 (page 77).

10. Cut two 1¼″ × 1¾″ sleeves from red velour fabric. Fold each in half, right side in and shorter edges matching. Sew shorter edges together to make a tube. Turn to right side.

11. Brush glue on the wrist section of each hand. Slip wrist into open end of sleeve. Press until glue is set.

12. Tack upper end of each sleeve to net bag at ear level of face.

FINISHING.

13. Brush mesh with a light coat of fabric stiffener. Let dry.

NET SANTA BOOT

The boot portion of this ornament is crafted from cardboard tubing and Styrofoam. The sculpted head is separate from the drawstring, which means that you can substitute a sticker or scrap face if you wish. It stands about 6″ tall.

MATERIALS AND TOOLS

painted modelling-compound Santa face, ¾″ across (see box), or sticker or scrap face

two painted modelling-compound hands, ⅜″ across × ¾″ long (see box)

2″ × 6″ coffee-dyed mesh or net (to coffee-dye, see box on page 71)

6″ × 6″ red fabric

16″ green cord for drawstring (to make twisted cord, see page 114)

two 12″ 6-mm white chenille stems

white wool roving

1½″-diameter cardboard tube

heavy-weight cardboard

1½″ × 1½″ Styrofoam block

aluminum foil

fabric stiffener

thick white tacky glue

glue applicator

paintbrush

stiff brush (for glue)

craft knife

DIRECTIONS

TO MAKE THE BOOT:

1. Mark a 3½″ section of cardboard tube, and cut it as precisely as you can with a craft knife.

2. Make two tracings of the actual-size boot-opening pattern. Match straight edge of one tracing to edge of tube and tape down. Cut on curved line through both layers with a craft knife. Remove tracing. Tape second tracing to one side of Styrofoam block, aligning straight edges. Using the craft knife, carve end of block into an inverted U shape for boot shoe.

3. Trace the actual-size sole pattern. Tape tracing to cardboard and cut out. Fit cardboard tube onto heel of sole so that opening faces towards toe. Tape at back heel.

4. Brush top surface of sole with glue. Set Styrofoam block on top so that curved end fits into tube cutout. Hold until glue is set. Let dry thoroughly.

5. Using cardboard sole as a guide, carve Styrofoam with a craft knife to shape boot toe. When you are finished, apply a bead of glue along all joins; let dry thoroughly.

6. Cut a 6″ × 12″ piece of aluminum foil. Place on a flat surface, shiny side down, and stand boot upright in middle. Wrap short edges of foil up around sides of boot, moulding it to boot contours. Wrap remaining foil up front and back of boot. Fold excess to inside.

TO MAKE THE NET BAG:

7 and 8. Same as Net Santa Sleigh, Steps 10 and 11 (page 77).

9. Apply a bead of glue to inside edge of boot top. With seam at the back of the boot, press raw edge of net tube against the glue. Hold until set.

TO MAKE THE HAT:

10. Same as Santa Starburst, Step 5 (page 52). Glue hat to top of head with seam at back.

TO ATTACH THE HEAD AND ARMS:

11. Glue head to front of boot so that head extends above boot top. Glue a tuft of roving to chin for beard.

12. Cut two 1½″ × 1¼″ sleeves from red velour fabric. Fold each in half, right side in and longer edges matching. Sew longer edges together to make a tube. Turn to right side.

13. Brush glue on the wrist section of each hand. Slip wrist into open end of sleeve. Press until glue is set. Glue each upper arm to the boot rim at the sides.

14. Bend a chenille stem to fit around the boot rim and up around the hat edge. Trim off excess. Glue in place, concealing hat and upper-arm raw edges. Twist remaining chenille stem around a pin three times to form a pom-pom. Cut off excess; then glue to tip of hat.

FINISHING:

15. Insert drawstring through casing so that ends emerge at back seam. Brush mesh with a light coat of fabric stiffener. Let dry.

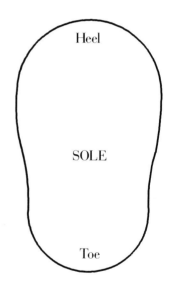

COTTON BATTING ANGEL

COTTON BATTING MOON AND STAR

Tinsel and stars decorate the soft batting robe of an old-fashioned Christmas angel. Yesteryear's homemaker relied on her own inventiveness and variety store notions to create festive decorations like these for her family. The pretty printed faces were cut from a wall calendar, and the delicate, ultra-thin batting was recycled from a worn-out Christmas tree drape. The angel is about 11" high, and the moon and star ornament is slightly smaller.

* * * * *

COTTON BATTING ANGEL

MATERIALS AND TOOLS

12″ × 18″ ultra-thin tea-dyed cotton batting or Christmas tree drape (to tea-dye, see box on page 84)

scrap face about 1¾″ across

two 12″ 6-mm gold tinsel stems

gold foil doily

self-adhesive gold foil stars

¼ yard jumbo silver loop trim with ribbon insertion for gathering

½ yard fine gold rope trim

heavy-weight cardboard or 4-ply posterboard

ice-cream stick

thick white tacky glue

clear arts-and-crafts glue

glue applicator

stiff brush (for glue)

glass-headed pins, in two colors

transparent ruler

Diagram 1

DIRECTIONS

TO MAKE THE ANGEL BODY:

1. Trace the actual-size angel pattern. Brush one side of the tracing with clear glue. Press it onto the cardboard, glue side down, and smooth out any wrinkles. When the glue is dry, cut out the angel body just inside the tracing line. Reinforce the figure by gluing an ice-cream stick extending from the head down.

2. Brush one side of the cardboard angel with tacky glue. Place the angel, glue side down, on a 6″ × 10″ piece of batting. Let dry; then trim away the excess batting ⅛″ beyond the cardboard edge. Cover the other side with batting and trim off the excess in the same way.

3. Use the glue applicator to run a thin bead of glue along the entire cardboard edge between the two batting edges. Press the batting edges together to seal them.

TO MAKE THE ROBE:

4. Cut a 7″ × 8″ piece of batting. Lay a ruler along one 7″ edge (top of robe). Following Diagram 1, pin-mark pleats at the points indicated. Use two different-colored pins to distinguish the top folds from the hidden folds. Fold the pleats as

marked, and then steam-press. Extreme precision is not necessary.

5. Apply a band of glue to the angel body ½″ below the neck edge. Position the pleated robe on top, and press firmly until the glue is set. Apply a second band of glue at the lower edge to anchor the skirt. Unfold the two outermost pleats to flare the skirt.

FINISHING AND TRIMS:

6. Shape the gold tinsel stems to conform to the outer edge of each wing, and trim off any excess. Apply a thin bead of glue around each wing edge, and position the shaped tinsel stem on it. Let dry thoroughly.

7. Glue a thin puff of batting to the head area, and glue the scrap face on top. Cut a small curved section from the foil doily, and glue it just below the neck for a collar.

8. Gather the silver loop trim into a tight circle by pulling the ribbon insertion at both ends. Tie ribbons in a knot to secure. Glue this halo to the back of the head. Tie the ribbon ends together to form a self-loop for hanging.

9. Affix foil stars to the wings and down the front of the robe. Cut one 7″ and one 8″ strand from gold rope trim. Glue the ends to the shoulders for a necklace.

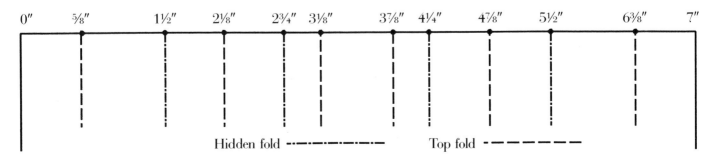

0″ ⅝″ 1½″ 2⅛″ 2¾″ 3⅛″ 3⅞″ 4¼″ 4⅞″ 5½″ 6⅜″ 7″

Hidden fold ------ Top fold -- -- --

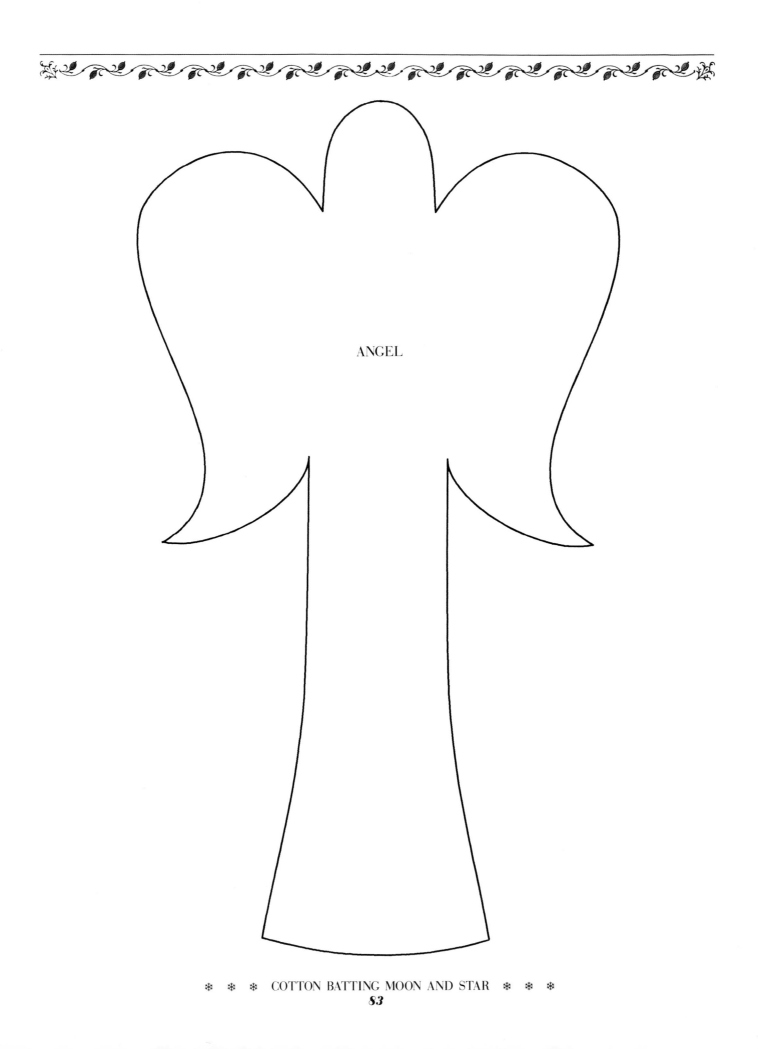

ANGEL

COTTON BATTING MOON AND STAR

Children will find this night-sky motif challenging to cut out and decorate. The tiny silver and gold stars are individually embossed from the wrong side, a technique you'll want to try for other projects as well. It stands about 7" high.

MATERIALS AND TOOLS

8" × 14" ultra-thin tea-dyed cotton batting or Christmas tree drape (to tea-dye, see box on page 84)

angel scrap face with wings, about 2" across

three 12" 6-mm gold tinsel stems

gummed gold and silver foil stars

heavy-weight cardboard or 4-ply posterboard

nylon thread

thick white tacky glue

glue applicator

stiff brush (for glue)

cotton swab

craft knife

awl

DIRECTIONS

1. Trace the actual-size moon-and-star pattern. Proceed as for Cotton Batting Angel, Step 1. Don't forget to cut out the interior section. *Older children can try using a craft knife if you provide supervision.*

2 and 3. Brush one side of the cardboard moon and star with glue. Place it, glue side down, on a 7" × 8" piece of batting. Proceed as for Cotton Batting Angel, Steps 2 and 3.

4. Shape two gold tinsel stems to conform to the edges of the crescent moon. Trim off and save the excess. Apply a thin bead of glue to moon edge, and position the shaped tinsel stems on it. Let dry thoroughly.

5. Bend the remaining tinsel stem into V shapes to fit between adjacent star points; trim off excess. Glue in place.

6. Glue the angel scrap to the batting star. Emboss the foil stars by turning each one upside down and pressing hard with a cotton swab from the middle out to each point. Glue the stars at random to the moon.

7. Use an awl to pierce a hole at top of moon. Run a 7" length of nylon thread through the hole, and tie the ends together for a hanging loop. You can also use a narrow metallic ribbon or cord.

MOON AND STAR

TREETOP SANTA

Santa figures with white batting coats were among the decorations nineteenth-century homemakers created using quilting scraps. This version is worked over a cardboard tube that fits on top of the Christmas tree. For a red-coated Santa, follow the hand-dying instructions in the box on page 90. Santa is about 13" tall.

❋ ❋ ❋ ❋ ❋

MATERIALS AND TOOLS

Santa sticker or scrap face, about 1¾" across

15" × 15" unbleached cotton batting

¾ yard white roving

⅓ yard black roving

two 12" 9-mm black chenille stems

12" 15-mm white chenille stem

12" 6-mm gold tinsel stem

12" green tinsel garland

small glass beads for belt

1¼"-diameter cardboard tube

beads for belt

3½" white tree

five 4" to 5" florist's sprigs

brown florist's tape

heavy-duty off-white thread

thick white tacky glue

glue applicator

stiff brush (for glue)

craft knife

wire cutters

DIRECTIONS

TO MAKE THE BODY:

1. Section off and pull out about one-third of the black roving fibres (about ¼″ diameter if compressed tight). Brush a black chenille stem with tacky glue. Wrap the black roving around it tightly from end to end until the entire length is covered. You may need to apply more glue as you wrap. Cover the other black stem in the same way. When the glue is dry, bend each stem in an **L** shape 1″ from the bottom to form feet.

2. Pull out about one-third of the white roving fibres. Brush the white chenille stem with tacky glue, and wrap tightly with the white roving to make arm piece.

3. Measure an 8″ length of cardboard tube, and cut with a craft knife. Slide the black legs inside the tube so that the top edges are even and the feet extend out the bottom. Glue the upper legs to the inside back of the tube.

4. Turn the tube so that the back side faces you. Measure down 2½″ from the top, and then mark a 1½″ horizontal line following the curve of the tube. Cut through the cardboard on this line with a craft knife. Insert the white arm piece into this slit so that tube and arms form a lowercase **T** shape. Glue in position and let dry. Pad this

armature by wrapping and gluing white roving, mummy-style, around the torso and shoulder areas.

TO MAKE THE SLEEVES:

5. Cut a 5″ × 12″ piece of batting. Fold it in half lengthwise; then cut a 1″ slit at the midpoint of the fold (Diagram 1).

6. Slip the batting over the armature so that the "head" pops through the slit and the arms are covered. Overlap and glue the edges together at the underarms.

7. Cut two 1½″ × 4½″ pieces of batting. Fold the long edges ¼″ to the wrong side and glue securely. Wrap these pieces around each coat sleeve at the wrist edge, and glue in place for cuffs. The hands should extend about 1″.

TO MAKE THE COAT:

8. Cut a 9″ × 11″ piece of batting. Use pins to mark the position of two 2″ armhole slits. Test-fit the position of the armhole slits against your Santa body before you cut them (Diagram 2).

9. Wrap the coat around the armature so that the arms correspond to the armhole slits and the right front is lapped over the left for a side closure. Fold the armhole edges in; bring the coat up and over the sleeve piece in back and up in front. Glue the coat "neck" to the cardboard tube.

FINISHING:

10. Pad the upper tube head area by wrapping and gluing roving

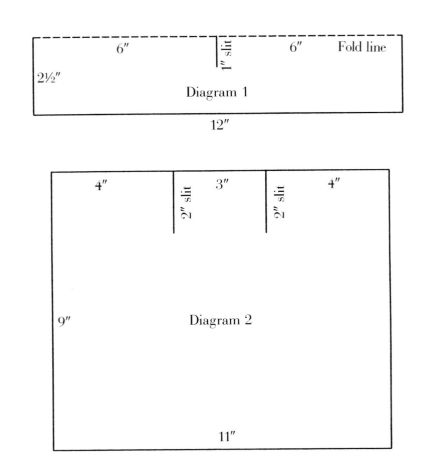

around it. Stuff extra roving under the coat to fill out any hollows in the chest and neck. Glue on the scrap face.

11. Trace the actual-size hood pattern. Tape the tracing to batting and cut out. Fold the hood in half and sew the ¼″ seam. Turn so that the seam is on the inside. Glue the hood to Santa's head with the seam at the back. Glue a band of roving around the edge.

12. String several glass beads on a double-strand of heavy-duty off-white thread. Tie the thread around Santa's waist for a belt. Arrange the garland around his neck, and glue at back. Shape the gold metallic stem diagonally across the coat.

13. Hold the florist's sprigs together, and wrap the lower ends with florist's tape. Bend Santa's left hand around the taped section and his right arm around the trunk of the miniature tree.

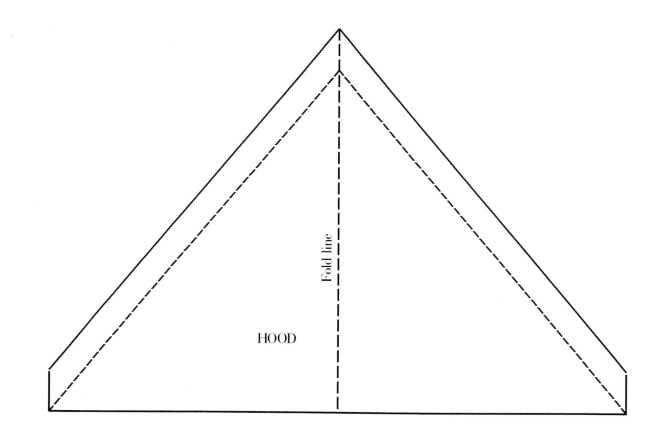

Fold line

HOOD

TWIN SANTAS

two painted chalkware Santa faces, ⅞" across (see page 29), *or* two sticker or scrap faces

12" × 12" unbleached cotton batting

12" × 12" red cotton batting (to hand-dye, see box that follows)

¼ yard white roving

¼ yard black roving

small amount red roving (to hand-dye, see box that follows)

two 12" 6-mm white chenille stems

two 12" 6-mm black chenille stems

two 12" 6-mm red chenille stems (to hand-dye, see box that follows)

4½" 20-mm pine chenille stem

two red berry pips

black felt

gold fabric paint

"washable" fabric glue

thick white tacky glue

glue applicator

medium and fine paintbrushes

*M*ake these antique Santa twins—one in a red coat, the other in white—out of batting scraps, wool roving, and pipe cleaners. Red dye provides the faded tint, and modern fabric ad-hesive creates the stiffened, sculpted look. The faces are chalkware, but you can also use a picture sticker or scrap face. Each Santa is about 6" tall.

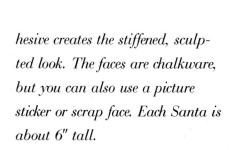

❋ ❋ ❋ ❋ ❋

DIRECTIONS

TO MAKE THE BODY:

1. Cut a 5″ length of white chenille stem. Section off and pull out about one-third of the white roving fibres (about ¼″ diameter if compressed tight). Brush the stem with tacky glue. Wrap white roving around it tightly from end to end until entire length is covered. You may need to apply more glue as you wrap.

2. Pull out about one-third of the black roving fibres. Brush a 12″ black chenille stem with tacky glue; then wrap it tightly with the black roving. When the glue is dry, bend the stem in half to make an inverted **V**. Make **L**-shaped bends ¾″ from each end to form feet.

3. Hold the black piece vertically with the feet at the bottom. Place the white piece across it about 1¼″ from the top, forming a lowercase **T** shape. Glue in this position and let dry. Pad this armature by wrapping and gluing white roving, mummy-style, around the torso, shoulders, and head.

TO MAKE THE SLEEVES:

4. Cut a 3″ × 5″ piece of white (or red) batting. Fold it in half lengthwise; then cut a ½″ slit at the midpoint of the fold (Diagram 1).

5. Slip the batting over the armature so that the head pops through the slit and the arms are covered. Overlap and glue the edges together at the underarms.

6. Hand-gather the sleeve edges and glue to the arms, pushing sleeves up slightly so that the "hands" extend. Bend contrasting chenille stems around the wrists, trim off excess, and glue in place for cuffs.

TO MAKE THE COAT:

7. Cut a 3¾″ × 5″ piece of white (or red) batting. Use pins to mark the position of two ½″ armhole slits. Test-fit the position of the armhole slits against your Santa body before you cut them. Trim the two lower corners, forming gentle curves (Diagram 2).

8. Bend a contrasting chenille stem to fit the coat edge between the **X**s, running it down the left side, across the bottom, and 1″ up the right side (Diagram 3). Using the glue applicator, apply a thin bead of glue to this edge. Position the stem on it and let dry thoroughly.

9. Wrap the coat around the armature, moulding the chenille stem trim to hug the body padding. As you adjust the coat, slip the top edges under the sleeve piece in front and back; you may need to turn under the edges at the armhole slits. Glue at the neck, armholes, and front overlap. Stuff extra matching roving under the coat to fill out the skirt.

HAND DYEING WITH ANTIQUE RED DYE

Dissolve ¼ teaspoon of fabric red dye, a drop of liquid detergent, and a pinch of kosher salt in 1 cup boiling water. Dip batting, chenille stems, and roving in the dye solution just long enough to color the pieces. Let them dry overnight on old, clean terry towels. *Be sure to wear rubber gloves while working with dye and keep the bowls and measuring spoons you use for dyes separate from those you use for cooking and baking.*

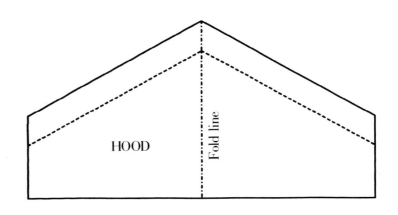

HOOD
Fold line

FINISHING AND TRIMS:

10. Glue the face in position; then add a tuft of white roving for the beard.

11. Trace the actual-size hood pattern. Tape the tracing to white (or red) batting and cut out. Fold the hood in half and sew the ¼″ seam. Turn so that the seam is on the inside. Place the hood on Santa's head with the seam at the back, and tuck the lower edge inside the shoulders. Glue in place.

12. Apply a bead of glue around the hood edges, and affix contrasting chenille stem trim as you did for cuffs.

13. Mix a small amount of fabric glue and water to achieve a light cream consistency. Brush the entire Santa with this mixture. It will dry to a semihard shell.

14. Cut the 4½″ pine stem in half. Wrap a pip stem around each pine stem so that the pips are at the top. Glue each sprig to a coat front, and bend Santa's arm up to clutch it.

15. Cut a ¼″ × 4½″ strip of black felt. Glue it around the waist for a belt. Dip a fine brush into gold fabric paint, and paint a buckle in front.

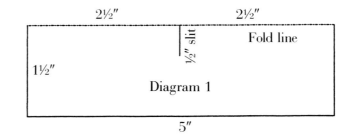

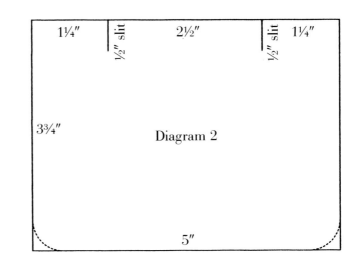

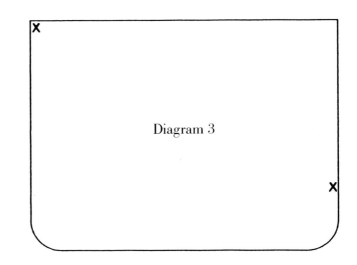

SAILOR SANTA

A recycled cardboard egg
carton is the secret ingredient in
creating this antique-looking sailboat. The textured surface spar-
kles with gold metallic paint and
glitter. The petite Santa skipper
on board can also be used alone
as a tree ornament or package tie-
on. The sailboat is 7" high, and
the Santa is a wee 3".

✳ ✳ ✳ ✳ ✳

SANTA SKIPPER

MATERIALS AND TOOLS

painted chalkware Santa face, ½"
across (see page 29), *or* a sticker or
scrap face

6" × 6" red cotton batting (to
hand-dye, see box on page 90)

6" red roving (to hand-dye, see box
on page 90)

6" white pipe cleaner

6" black pipe cleaner

black felt

thick white tacky glue

glue applicator

stiff brush (for glue)

embroidery scissors

DIRECTIONS

1. Cut a 5½" length of black pipe
cleaner. Bend it in half to form a
hairpin shape. Make L-shaped
bends ¼" from each end to form
feet. Glue the face to the top.
2. Cut a 3¼" length of white
chenille stem. Section off and pull
out about one-third of the red
roving fibres. Brush the stem with
tacky glue. Wrap the red roving
around it tightly, from end to end,
until the entire length is covered.
You may need to apply more glue as
you wrap.
3. Position the red arm piece
behind the black body to form a

lower-case T shape. Bend the arms
forward, and cross them in front in
a tight wrap. Pad this armature by
wrapping and gluing a small
amount of red roving, mummy-
style, around the torso. Glue a small
wad of roving to back of head.
4. Trace the actual-size coat
pattern. Tape the tracing to the red
batting and cut out. Cut the
armhole slits. Wrap the coat around
the Santa, slipping the arms
through the slits and covering the
head. Trim off the corners that hide
the face. Glue the coat in place. Pad

under the coat skirt with extra
roving if needed.
5. Trace the actual-size hood
pattern, and cut out from red
batting. Wrap the hood around the
face. Overlap the edges at the back
and glue in place.
6. Shape the remaining white pipe
cleaner around the face, and trim
off the excess. Using the glue
applicator, apply a thin bead of glue
around the face and press the
chenille in place. Cut a ⅛" strip of
black felt, and glue around the
waist for a belt.

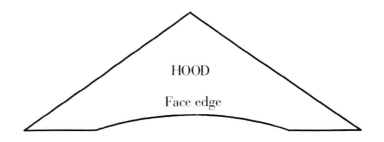

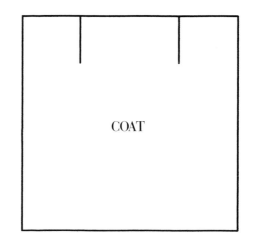

SAILBOAT

MATERIALS AND TOOLS

one cardboard egg carton, 1½-dozen size

one round tapered chopstick

very fine "stardust" glitter

1″ gold glitter star

28-gauge steel wire

gold metallic paint

thick white tacky glue

clear arts-and-crafts glue

glue applicator

paintbrush

stiff brush (for glue)

transparent ruler

jumbo paper clips

craft knife

coping saw

needle-nose pliers with built-in wire cutter

DIRECTIONS

1. Remove the lid from the egg carton. Trim away curved edges to make a large flat piece.

2. Trace the actual-size hull, jib, and mainsail patterns. Tape the tracings to the flat lid, and cut out on the marked lines. Use a craft knife and a transparent ruler to score the hull fold lines.

3. Fold the hull as indicated (the textured surface should appear on the outside). Brush tacky glue on the flaps, press them against the hull interior, and hold with jumbo paper clips until the glue is dry.

4. Measure a 6″ length of chopstick from the tapered end, and cut with a coping saw.

5. Cut a 3″ piece of 28-gauge steel wire. Using pliers, bend the wire into a hairpin shape and twist the ends together to create a loop. Using the glue applicator, apply a thick bead of tacky glue down the straight edge of the jib. Lay the chopstick mast on the glue, tapered end at the top; the chopstick will extend at the bottom. Slip the twisted wire ends between the jib and mast at the top for a hanging loop. Hold until glue is set.

6. Turn the main sail wrong side up. Apply a thick bead of glue down the long straight edge. Position the main sail on the mast, glue side down, about 1½″ below the top. Hold until set.

7. Apply glue to the interior of the hull, and place the lower end of the mast on it, as indicated on the pattern. Prop the hull open with a coin until the glue is dry.

8. Brush the hull, sails, and mast with gold metallic paint, and let dry.

9. Brush a light coat of clear glue over the sailboat, and sprinkle with very fine glitter. Glue a star to the top of the mast.

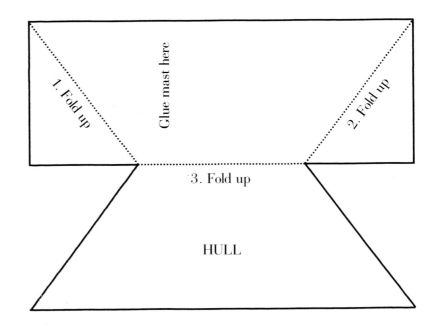

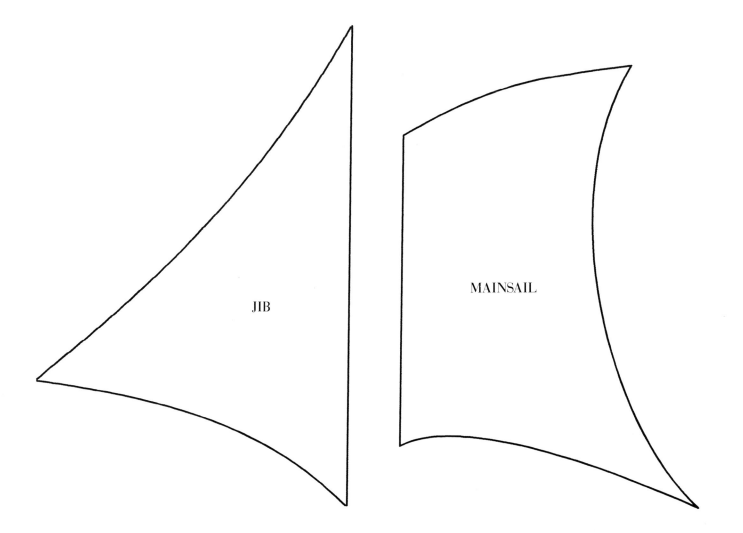

JIB

MAINSAIL

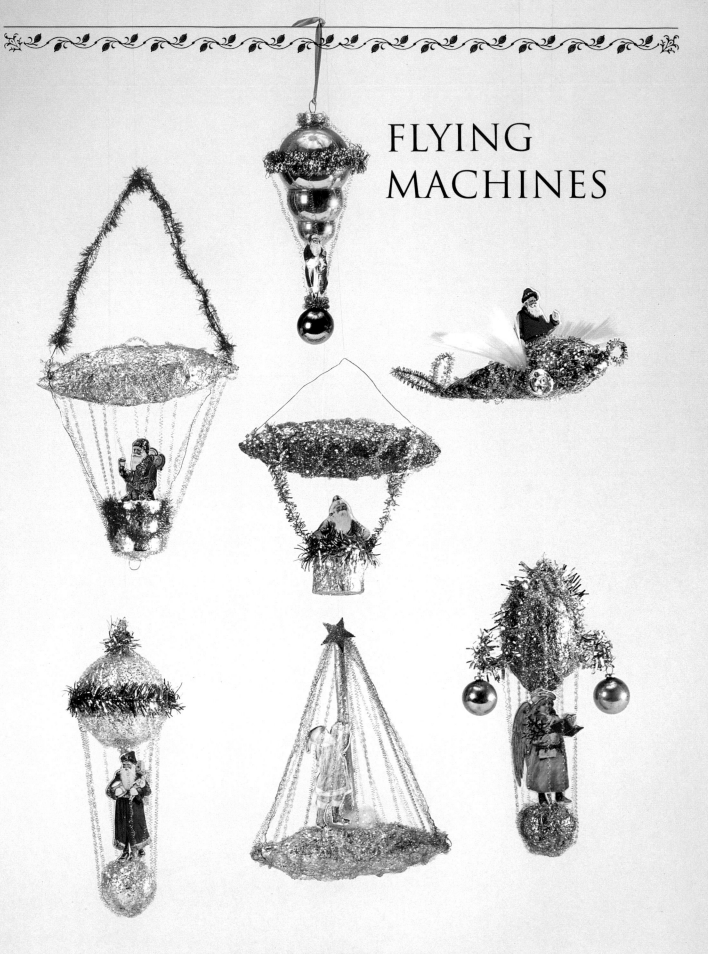

FLYING MACHINES

Here's a collection of real and fanciful flying machines for Santa to ride. All require similar techniques and materials, so you'll probably want to make several at a time. The papier-mâché hulls are covered with confectioner's foil and liquid glitter, giving them the look of antique hand-blown glass. Sizes range from 3½" to 8½" high.

❄ ❄ ❄ ❄ ❄

BASIC MATERIALS AND TOOLS

Santa or angel two-sided flat cardboard ornaments, 2" to 3" tall

9" × 9" sheets of confectioner's foil, assorted colors

silver and gold "stretch" crinkle wires, 22" each

opaque and sparkling glitter (sprinkle type) in assorted colors

assorted dollhouse garlands

28-gauge steel wire

clear iridescent fabric paint

silver iridescent liquid glitter

thick white tacky glue

clear arts-and-crafts glue

paintbrushes

stiff brush (for glue)

craft knife

needle-nose pliers with built-in wire cutter

awl

DIRIGIBLES

ADDITIONAL MATERIALS AND TOOLS

two papier-mâché dirigible hulls (see box on page 102)

16" 6-mm gold tinsel stem

1¼"-diameter cardboard tube

compass

masking tape

DIRECTIONS

TO MAKE THE BASKET:

1. Mark a 1¼" section of cardboard tube, and cut it as precisely as you can with a craft knife.

2. Use a compass to draw a 1¼"-diameter circle on cardboard. Cut out the circle, and set it on one end of the cut tube. Cut a 4¼" piece of masking tape. Wrap it around one end of the tube so that half the tape width adheres to the tube and half is free. Clip into the allowance every ⅜" all around. Press these tape "tabs" onto the cardboard circle to hold it in place.

TO DECORATE THE DIRIGIBLE AND BASKET:

3. Brush the papier-mâché hull with tacky glue. Wrap one foil sheet around the hull; crush the foil to shape and trim off any excess.

4. Cut a 4½" × 7½" piece of contrasting foil for the basket. Lay the foil on a flat surface, wrong side up. Brush the outside of the basket with tacky glue, and set it down on the foil. Carefully mould the foil up around the basket sides and then down inside.

5. Cut a 12" length of wire for a hanger. Use an awl to pierce a hole through each end of the dirigible. Thread each end of the wire into a hole, and "kink" the ends to secure them.

6. Brush the dirigible and the basket with iridescent fabric paint, which will lighten and "antique" the foil; let dry. Brush on the liquid glitter; let dry. Brush on a light coat of clear glue, and sprinkle with sparkling and opaque glitter.

7. Cut an 11" length of crinkle wire. Secure one end to the wire hanger near the kink. Wrap the crinkle wire in random fashion around the dirigible, stretching it as you go. When you reach the end, anchor it to the wire hanger.

RED DIRIGIBLE ONLY:

8. Use an awl to pierce two holes in the basket—one opposite the other—about ¼" from the top rim. Run a 16" gold tinsel stem through both holes so that equal lengths extend on each side. Bend each extending stem up. Wrap each end once around the dirigible, and secure with a twist.

9. Glue a 4" length of garland to the outside rim of the basket. Stand a Santa figure inside.

GREEN DIRIGIBLE ONLY:

10. Use an awl to pierce three holes in the basket—two in the sides, as in Step 8 above, and one in the bottom. Cut a 14" length of wire and bend it in half. Insert the bent

end into the basket and out the hole in the bottom. Use needle-nose pliers to open this protruding wire into a small ¼″ loop. Twist the wire several times to secure the loop.

11. Thread each loose wire end out the basket side holes and up through the holes in the dirigible. Twist the ends to the wire hanger to secure them.

12. Wrap a 9″ length of dollhouse garland twice around the outside of the basket, and glue it in place.

13. Select two 22″ crinkle wires. Twirl the end of one crinkle wire around the wire hanger close to the kink; crimp with your fingertips to secure it. Carefully stretch and wrap the crinkle wire around the dirigible and basket in successive passes until you reach the middle; anchor the crinkle wire on each pass in the wire loop at the bottom of the basket. To end off, secure the free end in this loop as well. Repeat with second crinkle wire, beginning from the other side.

14. Wrap crinkle wire and dollhouse garland around the wire hanger. Stand a Santa in the basket.

AIRSHIP

ADDITIONAL MATERIALS AND TOOLS

papier-mâché airship hull (see page 102)

6¾″ of ¼″ dowel

fiberfill (small amount)

silver glitter star

drill with ¹⁄₁₆″ bit

vise

DIRECTIONS

TO ASSEMBLE THE AIRSHIP:

1. Cover the papier-mâché hull with foil as for the Dirigibles, Step 3 (page 97). Use an awl to pierce a tiny hole in the top of the airship. Cut a small **X** across the hole with a craft knife.

2. Secure the dowel in a vise for drilling. Using a ¹⁄₁₆″ bit, drill a ½″ hole in one end.

3. Brush the undrilled end of the dowel with tacky glue, and insert it into the hull for a mast. Cut a 6″ × 2″ piece of foil. Brush the wrong side with tacky glue, and wrap it around the mast.

4. Cut a 2″ length of wire. Bend it into a hairpin shape, and twist the ends together in a tight spiral. Brush the spiraled section with glue, and insert it into the hole at the top of the mast.

5. Cut a 15″ length of wire. Use an awl to pierce a hole through each end of the airship. Thread the wire through one hole, and "kink" the end to secure it. Pass the wire up through the top mast loop and back down to the other side of the airship. Insert it into the hole, and kink it securely.

TO DECORATE THE AIRSHIP:

6 and 7. Same as Dirigibles, Steps 6 and 7 (page 97).

8. Arrange a small fluff of fiberfill around the base of the mast for a cloudlike cockpit. Stand a Santa figure in cockpit next to mast. Glue in position.

9. Same as Dirigibles, Step 13. To finish, glue a star to the top of the mast.

AIRPLANE

ADDITIONAL MATERIALS AND TOOLS

papier-mâché airplane hull (see box on page 102)

two 4″ spun glass bird tails

two 12″ 6-mm gold tinsel stems

two ½″ buttons

½″ brass finishing nail

masking tape

DIRECTIONS

TO ASSEMBLE THE AIRPLANE:

1. Trace the actual-size cockpit and wing-slot pattern. Tape the tracing around the papier-mâché airplane hull about 2″ from nose end (cockpit should be at the widest section of the hull). Cut into the hull on the marked lines with a craft knife. Remove the tracing paper and the cutout sections.

2. Cover the hull with foil as for the Dirigibles, Step 3 (page 97). Slice through the foil at the cockpit and wing slots, and fold the excess to the inside.

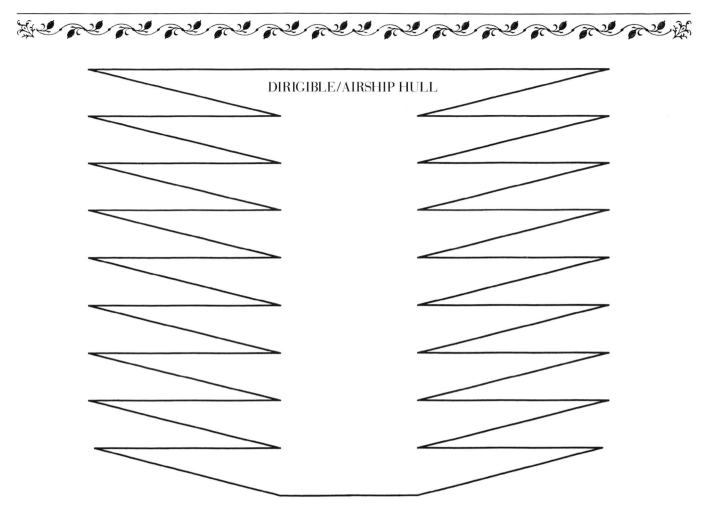

DIRIGIBLE/AIRSHIP HULL

TO DECORATE THE AIRPLANE:

3. Same as Dirigibles, Step 6.

4. Insert each bird tail into a wing slot. Select a Santa figure for the pilot, trim his legs and waist as necessary, and fit him into the cockpit. Press the figure down on the bird tail ends so that they fan out and tilt up. Glue in place.

5. Cut an 11″ length of crinkle wire. Glue one end to the inside cockpit. Wrap the crinkle wire randomly around the airplane, stretching it as you go.

6. Cut two 1½″ × 1½″ pieces of confectioner's foil. Wrap each one around a button. Glue the buttons to the airplane below the bird tail wings for wheels.

7. Cut a 6″ length of gold tinsel stem. Overlap the ends ½″ to form a circle, and twist to secure. Hold the circle in two hands. Twist your right hand up and your left hand down until the circle forms a figure-eight propeller. Twist once at the crossover to secure it.

8. Use an awl to pierce a small hole in the nose of the airplane. Insert the brass nail into the middle of the propeller. Brush the end of the nail liberally with tacky glue, and insert it into the nose.

9. Repeat Step 7 with a 9″ length of tinsel stem to form the tail fin. Glue it to the tail of the airplane. Elongate the loops slightly and bend them up.

10. Locate the hanging-cord hole in the Santa, and thread it with the cord of your choice.

GOLD HOT-AIR BALLOON

ADDITIONAL MATERIALS AND TOOLS

3″ Styrofoam ball

1½″ Styrofoam ball

7″ of ¼″ dowel

AIRPLANE
HULL

COCKPIT AND
WING SLOTS

5″ doll-making needle

drill with ⅟₁₆″ bit

vise

DIRECTIONS

1. Insert the doll-making needle straight through the core of each Styrofoam ball, and draw it out the other side.

2. Secure the dowel in a vise for drilling. Using a ⅟₁₆″ bit, drill a ½″ hole in the center of each end.

3. Work each dowel end into a ball, making additional passes with the doll-making needle to widen the holes if necessary. Each dowel end should be visible and even with the ball surface, and about 3½″ of dowel should show between balls. Remove both balls from dowel.

4. Select a 9″ × 9″ piece of confectioner's foil. Brush the large ball with glue. Roll the ball across the foil diagonally, from corner to corner; then crush excess foil to shape around it. Cut a 5½″ × 5½″ piece of foil, and cover the small ball in the same way.

5. Locate one dowel hole beneath the surface of the foil in the large ball. Break the foil open over this spot with a craft knife. Brush one end of the dowel liberally with tacky glue, and insert it into the ball, being careful not to break through the foil on the opposite side. Glue the other end of the dowel to the small ball in the same way. Cut a 3½″ × 2″ piece of foil. Brush the wrong side with tacky glue, and wrap it around the exposed dowel between the balls.

6. Locate the dowel ends under the foil. Use the tip of the needle to pierce through the foil at each predrilled hole.

7. Cut two 2″ lengths of wire. Bend each one into a hairpin shape, and twist the ends together in a tight spiral. Brush the spiraled sections with glue, and insert them into the holes at each dowel end.

8. Brush the balls and mast with clear iridescent fabric paint, which will lighten and "antique" the foil;

let dry. Brush on the liquid glitter; let dry. Brush the balls only with a light coat of clear glue, and sprinkle with sparkling and opaque glitter.

9. Cut an 11″ piece of crinkle wire. Secure one end to the wire loop on top of the large ball. Wrap the wire in random fashion around the balloon, stretching it as you go. Cut a 7″ piece of crinkle wire, and wrap the small ball in the same way.

10. Stand a Santa figure on the small ball and glue it in place.

11. Select a 22″ length of crinkle wire. Twirl the end around a wire loop, and crimp with your fingertips to secure it. Carefully stretch and wrap the crinkle wire evenly around the entire piece, anchoring it on each pass in the wire loops at the top and the bottom. When you reach the end, crimp to secure. Continue wrapping with an 11″ length of matching crinkle wire for a total of five complete passes.

12. Glue garland trim around the large ball and over the top loop.

PINK HOT-AIR BALLOON

ADDITIONAL MATERIALS AND TOOLS

3″ Styrofoam egg

1½″ Styrofoam ball

two small green glass balls

18″ gold metallic tinsel stem

7″ of ¼″ dowel

5″ doll-making needle

drill with 1/16″ bit

vise

DIRECTIONS

1. Insert the doll-making needle lengthwise through the Styrofoam egg, and draw it out the other end. Repeat to make a hole through the small ball.

2–10. Proceed as for the Gold Hot-Air Balloon, Steps 2–10, substituting the egg for the large ball. Use an angel figure in Step 10.

11. Cut a 7″ length of gold tinsel stem. Place the middle of the stem at the top of the egg. Bend the stem down around the egg; then curl up the ends. Glue it in place. Hang two green glass ball "weather meters" from each curl.

GLASS-BALL HOT-AIR BALLOON

ADDITIONAL MATERIALS AND TOOLS

3½″ three-tier novelty glass ball

1″ blue glass ball

12-mm gold loop garland

Santa scrap

plastic drinking straw

DIRECTIONS

1. Cut a 2″ length of drinking straw. Make eight short clips (about ⅛″ long) around the rim at one end. Apply a generous amount of tacky glue to the inside of the clipped rim. Press the bottom point of the novelty ornament into it, and hold until set.

2. Remove the hanger wire and cap from the small glass ball. Glue the lower end of the straw over the opening.

3. Cut a 2″ × 2″ piece of confectioner's foil. Brush the wrong side with clear glue, and wrap it, glue side down, around the straw.

4. Glue gold loop garland around the broadest tier of the "balloon." Trim off excess.

5. Cut a 2″ length of wire. Wrap it loosely around the base of the mast, and secure with tacky glue. Glue another wire to the top of the "balloon," just below the cap.

6. Select a 22″ length of crinkle wire. Twirl the end around the wire at the top of the balloon, and crimp it with your fingertips to secure it. Carefully stretch and wrap the crinkle wire evenly around the ornament about four times, anchoring it on each pass in the wire loops at the base of the mast and at the top of the ornament. The garland will help hold the crinkle wire in place.

7. Carefully slip the Santa scrap under the crinkle wire and glue it to the mast.

MAKING THE PAPIER-MÂCHÉ HULL

MATERIALS AND TOOLS

1¼"-diameter cardboard tube (from giftwrap roll)

¼" quilter's tape (or thin strips cut from masking tape)

white flour

newspaper

water

mixing bowl

measuring cup

spoon

baking rack

craft knife

DIRECTIONS

1. Measure a 5½" length of cardboard tube, and cut with a craft knife. Trace the actual-size dirigible/airship or airplane pattern. Wrap the tracing paper pattern around the tube, and secure it with tape. (The pattern markings will not align exactly, but that's okay.) The tube should extend a bit on each side.

2. Use scissors to cut into the cardboard tube on the marked lines. Remove the tracing paper.

3. At each end of the tube, bring the cut ends together into a point. Hold the shape with your fingers as you wrap with ¼" quilter's tape. Extreme precision is not

necessary; simply taper the form at each end.

4. Measure ¼ cup warm water and pour into a mixing bowl. Add ⅓ cup flour and stir to form a smooth paste.

5. Tear (don't cut) newspaper into narrow strips. Dip one strip into the mixture to coat it, and smooth away the excess paste with your fingers. Wrap the moist strip randomly around the cardboard form, smoothing it as you go. Keep adding strips, overlapping them around the form, until the hull is coated with several layers. Let dry on a baking rack 24 to 48 hours until hard.

Taper the ends of the hull, and secure with ¼" quilter's tape (Step 3).

Pull the moistened newspaper strip through your fingers to remove the excess flour-water mixture (Step 5).

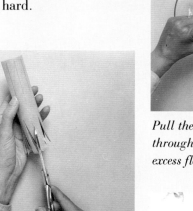

Tape the pattern around the tube, and cut on the marked lines (Steps 1 and 2).

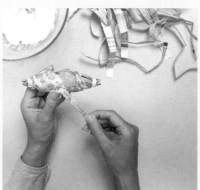

Wrap the strips randomly around the cardboard hull until it is completely covered (Step 5).

CHENILLE SANTAS

These perky red Santas were made in Japan during the early twentieth century. The thick-and-thin chenille stems are bendable and poseable. Many old Santas of this type are faded to a muted orangy pink, an effect you can achieve with red fabric dye. Each Santa is about 6" high.

✻ ✻ ✻ ✻

CHENILLE SANTA GARLAND

String this garland in a doorway or across a mirror or mantel. The Santas are smaller than the individual chenille Santa ornaments. They are joined by tiny Japanese trees. The garland is about 44" long.

✻ ✻ ✻ ✻

BASIC MATERIALS AND TOOLS

½ yard red 3″ bump chenille (to hand-dye white chenille, see box on page 90)

painted chalkware face, ½″ across (see page 29)

white wool roving

12″ 6-mm white chenille stem

short pine stem or miniature tree

thick white tacky glue

glue applicator

needle-nose pliers with built-in wire cutter

DIRECTIONS

1. For each Santa, cut one "four-bump" length and one "one-bump" length from chenille.
2. Bend the longer piece in half. Hold it vertically, with the bend at the top. Hold the shorter piece against it, just below the top pair of bumps, to form a lowercase **T** shape. Bend the short piece around the main stem, crossing the ends at the back for a tight wrap. You have just made a body with arms.
3. Glue a painted chalkware face to the front of the figure above the arms. Shape the white chenille stem around the face, and trim off the excess. Using the glue applicator, apply a bead of glue around the face. Place the shaped chenille stem on top and press until set. Glue a tuft of white roving to chin for beard.
4. Wrap Santa's right "hand" around a short pine stem or tree.

ADDITIONAL MATERIALS AND TOOLS FOR GARLAND

4¼ yards red 3″ bump chenille

4″ × 4″ pale pink cotton or knit fabric

3″ × 3″ thin batting

eight 6″ white pipe cleaners

fifteen 1½″ trees

fifteen ⅜″ wooden green or brown barrel beads

brown fine-point permanent marking pen

powder rouge

quilter's stencil plastic

marking pencil

DIRECTIONS

1. Cut one "18-bump" length of chenille. From the remaining chenille, cut 16 "two-bump" pieces.
2. Bend a "two-bump" piece in half. Hold it vertically, with the bend at the top. Hold the second bump in the long chenille strand against this body horizontally so that the widest parts of the bumps cross each other to form a + sign. Bend the horizontal bump around the body stem, crossing the ends at the back for a tight wrap. Repeat this step until you have a string of 16 bodies with arms. To make hanging loops, bend the bump at each end of the garland back on itself and twist several times.
3. Place the Santa strand on a flat surface with the crossed-arm wraps facing up. Set a tree between two Santas under the narrow section of the strand. Wrap the strand around the tree stem, crossing the ends in the back as above. Repeat this step to add all 15 trees.
4. Use pliers to bend each tree stem into a small loop. Fit the loop into a bead and glue it in place.

TO MAKE THE FACES:

5. Trace the actual-size face and pad patterns onto stencil plastic, and cut out. Using the plastic patterns and a marking pencil, mark 16 faces on pink fabric and 16 pads on batting. Cut out all pieces.
6. Using the glue applicator, apply a bead of glue around the edge of each face on the wrong side. Center a pad inside the glue line; then position the face on a Santa, glue side down, so that the lower face covers the middle arm join. Press firmly until glue is set.
7. Cut each white pipe cleaner in half. Bend each piece to match the curved face outline; trim off any excess. Apply a thin bead of glue to each face edge. Position the shaped pipe cleaner on it and press firmly. When the glue is dry, you can bend the pipe cleaners further to give the faces dimension.
8. Use a brown fine-point pen to dot in eyes on the faces. Brush the cheeks with rouge. Glue small tufts of roving to the chins for beards.

TABLETOP DECORATIONS

❊ ❊ ❊ ❊ ❊ ❊ ❊ ❊

Victorian households believed more was better when decorating for Christmas. Copious evergreen roping, a Christmas tree laden with ornaments and sweets, and centerpieces of candied fruits were the mainstays of holiday decorating. The manufacture of novelty Santa Clauses, miniature reindeer, and sleds inspired homemakers to drape batting on tabletops and mantels and create their own Christmas vignettes. Setting up these tableaux became a yearly holiday ritual that was as much a part of the festivities as Christmas Day itself.

The passion for sweets invariably led to decorative merchandising containers that could double as display pieces. During the holiday season, confectionery shops sold candies in sculpted cardboard containers with lift-off lids. Whimsical batting Santas, scrap figures, or tiny Christmas trees were glued on top for a candy package children found absolutely irresistible. Santas moulded of papier-mâché intrigued little fingers with their lift-off bodies—hard candies and chocolates lay waiting in the boots. Other packaging innovations included slippers, chimneys, sleds, and motorcars. They made charming hostess gifts, for in addition to presenting the sweets, they could be set

among the home's already effusive decorations. Old candy containers are highly collectible today; unfortunately, not many have survived as they were considered throwaways once the candy was consumed.

Other manufactured items also built on the Christmas theme. Children's books, puzzles, and board games were no different in concept from those sold throughout the year, but pictures of Santa Claus on the covers gave them special holiday appeal. To the young children who witnessed the profusion of Santa images flooding their own and neighbors' homes, it must have seemed as if the whole world was conspiring to welcome Santa Claus.

Of course, Santa never did stay very long—a fact for which mothers, no doubt, made secret thanksgiving. The ardent attention yesteryear's families lavished on holiday decorating lasted but a few weeks, from Advent up to Christmas Day, when all ages celebrated with joyful abandon. Vestiges of their merriment linger on in the old figures, candy containers, and toys of Christmas that remain. The replicas created here capture the essence of yesteryear's decorations, although the attraction they held in their original settings we can only wonder at now.

FEATHER TREE CONTAINERS
AND SANTA PULLING A SLED

Use these petite candy containers as place setting favors or alongside other decorations in a tabletop display. The round cardboard boxes are lined with rice paper and covered with giftwrap. Each is topped with a 6" feather tree trimmed with miniature ornaments or pips. Several make a woodsy backdrop for a sled-tugging Santa, inspired by a 1930s German-made piece. Original figures had papier-mâché heads, hands, and boots, but this interpretation uses a contemporary modelling compound that bakes hard in the oven and takes a paint finish. The rustic sled with natural twig sides can hold candies, small gifts, or toys. The entire piece is 10½" long. The 9" Santa can be made separately for other projects as well.

✳ ✳ ✳ ✳

MATERIALS AND TOOLS FOR EACH

medium-weight cardboard

giftwrap

rice paper

two 12″ 20-mm pine chenille stems

brown ½″ florist's tape

wick tab

miniature trims, such as red berry pips, glass balls, and birthday cake candle

28-gauge beading wire (to attach candle)

navy sewing thread

hot-glue gun

white glue

stiff brush (for glue)

mechanical pencil

transparent ruler

compass

craft knife

masking tape

wax paper

small jar or dish

DIRECTIONS

TO MAKE THE CANDY CONTAINER:

1. Use a compass to draft a 2″-diameter circle (label **T** for top) and a 1⅞″-diameter circle (label B for bottom) on cardboard. Using a transparent ruler and a craft knife, measure and score one ¾″ × 6¾″ strip (label T) and one 1⅝″ × 6⅜″ strip (label B) on cardboard. Cut

out all four pieces with scissors.

2. Affix masking tape to one long edge of strip B so that half the tape width is on B and half is free. Cut off tape ends even with B.

3. Clip into the tape allowance every ¼″ along entire edge to make tabs. Beginning at one end of the strip, butt the taped edge of strip B against the edge of circle B and fold the first tab onto the circle. Gently curve strip B around circle B, butting the edges and folding successive tabs onto circle B as you go.

4. When you reach the starting point, overlap the strip ends and tape them securely. You have just made the candy container bottom. Repeat steps 2–4 with circle T and strip T to make top.

TO LINE THE CANDY CONTAINER:

5. On rice paper, draft a 1⅞″-diameter circle (T), a 1¾″-diameter circle (B), a 1¼″ × 6¾″ strip (T), and a 3⅛″ × 6⅜″ strip (B). Cut out all pieces.

6. Make ½″-deep clips ¼″ apart along one long edge of each strip.

7. Squeeze some white glue into a small jar or dish, and thin with water until it reaches a heavy-cream consistency. Brush the interior wall and floor edge of candy container B with glue mixture. Position strip B inside the container so that the straight edge aligns with rim and the clipped allowance extends onto floor. Working quickly but systematically, smooth the lining into place over the wet glue, one section at a time, with your fingertips. Press the lining down

into the crevice, and ease the clipped tabs onto floor, overlapping them to accommodate the curve.

8. Brush the interior floor, including tabs, with glue mixture. Place lining circle B onto floor and smooth in place. Repeat Steps 7 and 8 with circle T and strip T to line candy container top.

TO PAPER THE CONTAINER EXTERIOR:

9. On wrong side of printed giftwrap, draft a 1⅞″-diameter circle (T), a 1¾″-diameter circle (B), a 1¾″ × 6¾″ strip (T), and a 3⅝″ × 6⅜″ strip (B). Cut out all pieces. Reinsert the compass point into the center of circle T to make a small pinhole.

10. Brush the exterior wall of candy container B with glue mixture. Lay strip B, centered, onto the gluey area so that ½″ extends beyond the rim and lower edge. Wrap the strip around the container, smoothing it in place. Overlap and glue ends.

11. Clip into the lower allowance every ¼″ to make tabs. Brush the edge of container bottom with glue mixture. Bend the tabs onto the gluey area, overlapping them to accommodate the curve. Brush the entire bottom exterior, including tabs, with glue mixture. Smooth circle B on top.

12. Clip into upper allowance every ¾″. Brush top inside edge of container with glue. Bend these large tabs onto the wet glue all around, and smooth into place. Repeat steps 10–12 to paper the container top.

13. Place cover on candy container. Set on wax paper on a flat surface, and lay a second sheet of wax paper on top. Weight with a heavy book overnight or until dry.
Note: To prevent warpage, finish steps 1–13 in one session.

TO MAKE THE TREE:

14. Cut two pine stems into one 6½″ and six 2¾″ sprigs. Hold the long stem so that the needles point up. Beginning at the bottom, wrap this long stem tightly with brown florist's tape; unwind the tape directly from the roll and stretch it as you wrap.

15. When 1½″ of the stem is wrapped, place the bottom end of a short sprig (make sure needles point up) against the long stem. Wrap the tape over the end of the sprig to secure it to the base stem. Add a second short sprig, then a third short sprig, making a complete wrap after each one. Bend the three sprigs away from the main stem.

16. Carry the tape up over the nearest sprig, and continue wrapping the main stem for 1″. Add the three remaining sprigs, one by one, as before. Then wrap the tape back down the stem, stopping ½″ from the end. Cut the tape and end off.

FINISHING:

17. Set the candy container on a hard, flat surface. Examine the cover to locate the tiny hole made by the compass point. Use a craft knife to cut a small **X** across this point. Insert the wrapped stem of the feather tree into the **X**, and push through until ⅜″ protrudes on the

inside lid.

18. Straighten the four corners of a wick tab. Apply hot glue to the inside lid around the tree stem. Slide the wick tab over the stem end, and hold until the glue sets.

19. Decorate the feather tree with miniature ornaments. Glass ornaments and jingle bells are tied to the branches with navy sewing thread (ask a partner to help you). Red berry pips with wire stems simply twist onto the branches. To make the candle holder, cut a 14″ length of 28-gauge wire. Bend it in half, and then twist to form a spiral. Coil this doubled strand around a narrow paintbrush handle five to seven times. Fit a birthday cake candle into the coil, and twist the remaining wire around the top of the tree.

SANTA

MATERIALS AND TOOLS

two-piece antique or reproduction metal Santa chocolate mould, face approximately 1¼″ across

½ lb. modelling compound

2″ × 3″ section of white rabbit hair pelt

9″ × 12″ dark royal blue felt

9″ × 12″ red felt

ultra-thin white cotton batting or Christmas tree drape

1″ × 1″ × 2″ balsa wood

two 18″ stems of 18-gauge florist's wire

3″ 20-mm pine chenille stem

red berry pip

dark-colored heavy-duty thread

black, Caucasian skin tone, red, rose, slate blue, and white acrylic paints

water-based antique finish

water-based clear matte finish

thick white tacky glue

paintbrush

stiff brush (for glue)

toothpick

small scissors or new single-edge razor blade

wire cutters

oven

baking rack

kitchen knife

DIRECTIONS

TO MAKE THE HEAD, HANDS, AND BOOTS:

1. Cut one 3″, two 4″, and two 5″ lengths from florist's wire stems.

2. Unclamp the chocolate mould and separate the halves. Roll a golf ball–size piece of modelling compound, and press it into the face section of the front half. Press firmly to pick up all the features. Mould the back of the head into a rounded shape with your fingers. Carefully remove the head from the mould. Insert the 3″ wire into the neck, leaving a 2″ extension.

3. Roll a quarter-size piece of modelling compound; then divide into two balls for hands. Roll each

ball into a short sausage about 1½" long. Slightly flatten two-thirds of the sausage to form a hand. Compress the remaining third to suggest a wrist. With a knife, score four lines on hand to suggest fingers. Cut one end finger shorter for thumb, remembering to switch thumb position for right and left hands.

4. Cup each hand slightly. Poke a toothpick through the middle of the left fist to make a hole for pine sprig. Insert a 4" wire into the end of each wrist, leaving a 3" extension.

5. Roll a golf ball–size piece of modelling compound; then divide into two balls for boots. Use your fingers to mould an L-shaped boot about 1¼" long, 1¾" high, and ⅝" thick. Press in on the "arch" of the foot with a straight-edged ruler to form the boot heel. Insert a 5" wire into each boot top, leaving a 4" extension.

6. Bake the head, hands, and boots immediately in a 275°F (135°C) oven for 20 minutes, or as suggested in the modelling compound package instructions. Set on a rack to cool.

7. Paint the face and hands Caucasian skin tone. Paint the eyebrows, moustache, and almond-shaped eyes white. Paint the boots black. Use a narrow brush and black paint mixed with red to outline the eyelids and fill in the score lines between the fingers. Paint the lips red. Paint the irises blue. Brush the cheeks with rose. Wash out the brush when you change colors. If you find you need to apply two coats for good

coverage, be sure to let the paint dry between coats.

8. Dilute 1 part antiquing with 1 part water. Brush onto head and hands, allowing mixture to pool in crevices. Smooth out any noticeable drips with a dry brush. Let dry.

9. Brush all pieces, including boots, with water-based matte finish. Work slowly so that bubbles don't form. Let dry thoroughly.

TO MAKE THE PANTS:

10. Cut two 3½" × 4¾" pants legs from blue felt. Fold each piece in half, shorter edges matching. Sew shorter edges together in a ⅛" seam to make a tube. Do not turn.

11. Insert a boot into pants leg so that only the top of the boot and the wire are visible. Brush glue around the top edge of the boot. Gather the pants leg around the boot, pressing the felt into the glue. Tie with dark-colored heavy-duty thread; let glue dry. Turn the pants leg right side out, bringing it up over the wire. Repeat for the second leg.

TO MAKE THE JACKET AND HOOD:

12. Trace the actual-size jacket, sleeve, and hood patterns. Cut out one jacket, two sleeves, and one hood from red felt. Cut front and neck openings, as indicated on jacket pattern.

13. Place sleeves on jacket so that dots and edges match. Sew with ⅛" seam. Fold jacket in half along neck opening, right sides facing, and sew underarm and side seams. Fold hood in half and sew back seam. Turn all pieces right side out.

ASSEMBLY AND FINISHING:

14. Stand the balsa-wood block vertically on work surface. Using a craft knife, trim off each corner diagonally to create an octagonal torso.

15. Push leg wires into one end of block for about 1". Insert arm wires into sides. Insert head into top. Remove all wires, brush with tacky glue, and reinsert.

16. Cut a ⅜" × 15" strip from white batting. Beginning at jacket neck, brush tacky glue down left front, around lower hem, and up right front, one edge at a time. Set batting strip in place after each application, mitring at lower front corners. Put coat on figure and glue at back of neck.

17. Put hood on head. Adjust so that curved section grazes forehead and point comes down over coat in back. Glue in place. Cut a ⅜" × 6¼" strip from white batting, and glue to lower edge of hood.

18. Trace the actual-size beard/moustache pattern. Transfer pattern to skin side of rabbit hair pelt. Cut out from wrong side with small scissors or a new single-edge razor blade, carefully separating hairs so that you cut skin only. Glue to face.

19. Wrap the pip stem around the 3" pine stem so that the pip is at the top. Insert end of sprig into Santa's left hand.

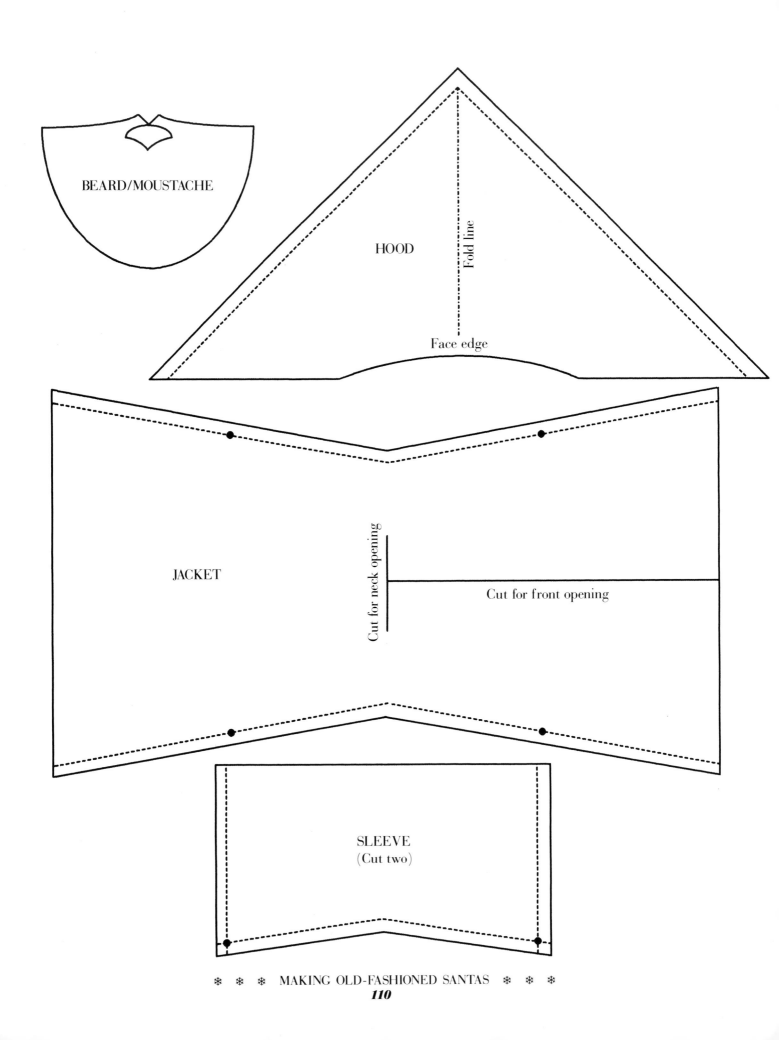

BEARD/MOUSTACHE

HOOD

Fold line

Face edge

JACKET

Cut for neck opening

Cut for front opening

SLEEVE
(Cut two)

SLED AND BASE

MATERIALS AND TOOLS

3¼" × 24" × ⅜" balsa wood

3¾" × 10½" × ⅜" plywood (for base)

small bundle of twigs, ¼" to ½" in diameter

18" white cord

5" tapered bottlebrush tree

small toys and animals

white opaque glitter

white sparkling glitter

black, brown, and white acrylic paints

water-based antique finish

acrylic modelling paste

thick white tacky glue

clear arts-and-crafts glue

glue applicator

stiff brush (for modelling paste and glue)

craft knife

coping saw

120-grit sandpaper

awl

DIRECTIONS

1. On balsa wood, measure and mark one 2½" × 4¼" rectangle (sled floor) and two 2" × 2½" rectangles (sled front and back). Cut out with coping saw. Sand edges lightly.

2. Place sled floor on work surface with short ends at top and bottom. Measure down ⅜" from the middle of the top edge, and mark with the point of a pencil. Pierce through this mark with an awl to make rope hole.

3. Trace the actual-size runner pattern twice. Tape each tracing to remaining balsa wood. Go over traced lines with a pencil, pressing firmly to leave indentation in wood. Remove tracings and cut out both runners with a craft knife.

4. Dilute approximately 2 tablespoons of antique finish with 1 tablespoon of water. Stir in a drop of black paint. Test the stain on a scrap of balsa wood—the color should match the charcoal-brown of the twigs. Add more black paint, one drop at a time, if needed. Brush stain on sled floor, front, back, and runners, and let dry.

5. From the twigs you have gathered, cut eight straight sections, each 4½" to 5" long, using the coping saw.

TO ASSEMBLE THE SLED:

6. Place stained sled floor on flat surface with rope hole at right. Using glue applicator, apply a bead of tacky glue along one 2½" edge of sled back. Hold sled back upright, and press gluey edge down along left edge of floor. Apply glue to one 2½" edge of sled front. Press gluey edge onto floor about ⅝" from right edge (rope hole should be to right of sled front). Hold both pieces until set.

7. When glue is thoroughly dry, tip sled back so that floor is perpendicular to work surface. Apply a bead of glue to 2" sides; then lay four twigs across the span. Arrange the twigs with spaces between them; let set until dry. Turn sled to opposite side, and glue remaining twigs in same way.

8. Turn sled over. Brush top edges of runners with glue, and position on floor bottom with side edges matching. Be sure the curved section of the runners points towards the front (rope-hole edge). Hold until set.

FINDING MINIATURES

In your search for miniature toys and animals to fill a tabletop sled, don't overlook broken or damaged items. You can always layer small treasures so that broken parts are hidden from view—once you've worked out an arrangement, just glue in place. Bargain sources include garage and rummage sales, and you're bound to find hidden treasures in your household junk drawer. Tell your children what you're after, and they're sure to contribute choice finds culled from their toy crates.

TO MAKE THE BASE:

9. Paint plywood base black; let dry. Brush top with modelling paste, allowing excess to drip down sides as snow; let dry. Paint top white; let dry.

FINISHING:

10. Fold cord in half, and slip loop through rope hole. Secure with a slip knot. Tie free ends together.

11. Stand Santa and sled on base, and mark positions lightly with a pencil. Apply tacky glue generously to soles of boots and bottom of runners, and glue in place. Slip rope over Santa's right arm.

12. Brush clear glue lightly on hat, coat, boots, sled, and base. Sprinkle white and opaque glitter onto gluey areas to resemble snow. Let dry; then brush off excess. Fill sled with tree and small toys.

RUNNER BLADE

SANTA'S MOTORCAR

A modern twentieth-century Santa trades in his sleigh and reindeer for a dapper motorcar. This motorcar is assembled from posterboard and then decorated with foil giftwrap, stars, and white chenille. The gold foil "Merry Christmas" script and Santa's face mask were purchased at a bakery-supply shop. For a tabletop display, fill the rumble seat with candy, small gifts, or holiday greenery. The car is 8" long, and the separate poseable Santa stands 9" tall.

* * * * *

SANTA

MATERIALS AND TOOLS

plastic Santa mask, about 1½″ across

½ lb. modelling compound

9″ × 12″ dark royal blue felt

9″ × 12″ red felt

1⅞″ × 7″ white felt

⅜″ × 8″ black felt

1″ × 1″ × 2″ balsa wood

two 18″ stems of 18-gauge florist's wire

small plastic holly sprig

heavy-duty thread

black, Caucasian skin tone, and red acrylic paints

water-based antique finish

water-based clear matte finish

thick white tacky glue

medium and fine paintbrushes

stiff brush (for glue)

toothpick

wire cutter

sharp knife

oven

baking rack

DIRECTIONS

TO MAKE THE HEAD, HANDS, AND BOOTS:

1. Cut one 3″, two 4″, and two 5″ lengths from florist's wire stems.

HOW TO MAKE A TWISTED CORD

Here's how to make a twisted cord to use as a drawstring, a tie-on belt, or a sled rope: Cut two strands of pearl cotton, each two-and-a-half times longer than the desired finished size. Hold one end of this double-strand, and have a partner hold the other. Face each other; then step back so that the cord is suspended between you. Begin twisting your end clockwise, and have your partner do the same. When you feel the cord tensing up, grasp the middle of the cord with your free hand, step in towards your partner, and allow the strand to relax. It will kink at the middle and the ends will begin to twirl together into a tight spiral. Hand your end to your partner to hold, while you guide the spiraling to make sure it is even. When the spiraling is completed, tie each end in an overhand knot to secure the twists. Trim and fluff out the ends to form tassels.

---

2. Roll a golf ball-size piece of modelling compound, and press it into the mask from the wrong side. Remove the head from mask. Carefully slice off the bottom third of head (this will allow the beard to extend over the front of the jacket). Insert the 3″ wire into the neck, leaving a 2″ extension.

3–6. Same as Santa Pulling a Sled, Steps 3–6 (page 109). You may wish to make the motorcar horn at this time; see Steps 34 and 35 (page 117) for directions.

7. Paint the hands Caucasian skin tone. Paint the boots black. Using a fine brush, apply black paint mixed with red to the score lines between the fingers. Wash out the brush when you change colors. If you find you need to apply two coats for good coverage, be sure to let the paint dry between coats.

8. Dilute 1 part antiquing with 1 part water. Brush onto hands, allowing mixture to pool in crevices. Smooth out any noticeable drips with a dry brush. Let dry.

9. Brush hands and boots with water-based matte finish. Work slowly so that bubbles don't form. Let dry thoroughly.

TO MAKE THE PANTS:

10 and 11. Same as Santa Pulling a Sled, Steps 10 and 11 (page 109).

TO MAKE THE JACKET AND HOOD:

12 and 13. Same as Santa Pulling a Sled, Steps 12 and 13 (page 109), except do not cut front opening.

ASSEMBLY AND FINISHING:

14 and 15. Same as Santa Pulling a Sled, Steps 14 and 15 (page 109).

16. Cut white felt into three ⅝″ × 7″ strips. Glue one strip around lower edge of jacket. Put jacket on figure, and glue to back of neck and down front. Cut a 3″ strip and glue down front. Glue black felt strip around waist for belt.

17. Put hood on head. Adjust so that curved section grazes forehead and point comes down over coat in back. Glue in place. Glue remaining 7″ white felt strip around lower edge of hood.

18. Insert end of holly sprig into Santa's left hand.

MOTORCAR

MATERIALS AND TOOLS

heavy-weight cardboard or 4-ply posterboard

red foil giftwrap

coordinating giftwrap (to line inside of car)

dark green and gold confectioner's foil

two 2½″ pieces baker's "Merry Christmas" gold foil script

gold foil self-adhesive stars

two small foil holiday stickers (for grille and back bumper)

three 12″ 15-mm white chenille stems

one 12″ 6-mm white chenille stem

3¼″, 4″, and 4¼″ lengths of ¼″ dowel

four ¾″ No. 15 brass finishing nails

8″ × 8″ coarse brown wool

green pearl cotton, size 3

stainless steel cake-decorating tip

modelling compound

black acrylic paint

thick white tacky glue

clear arts-and-crafts glue

hot-glue gun

stiff brush (for glue)

mechanical pencil

transparent ruler

¼″-diameter hole punch

jumbo paper clips

tweezers

craft knife

wire cutter

drill with 1/16″ bit

vise

coping saw

awl

self-healing cutting mat

transparent tape

removable transparent tape

DIRECTIONS

1. Using a transparent ruler and a mechanical pencil, trace the actual-size patterns for the body front, body back, chassis, and hood.

2. Using removable transparent tape, secure the individual tracings, right side up, to the cardboard or posterboard. Using a transparent ruler and a craft knife, carefully score all solid and dash lines, pressing the knife through the tracing paper and into the board.

3. When scoring is complete, lift off the tracing patterns. Cut with scissors on the solid lines. Retape the patterns on the board, and use a hole punch to cut the small circles for axle holes.

TO ASSEMBLE THE MOTORCAR:

4. Repunch each axle hole two or three times, shifting the position of the hole punch to enlarge each hole slightly. Test-fit the dowel in each hole. The dowel should fit snugly, without any movement.

5. Fold the body front and back on the prescored fold lines. Brush clear glue on the facing side of each flap. Position each flap against a side section, forming an open box. Hold each join secure with jumbo paper clips until dry.

6. Fold the chassis flaps on the score lines. Turn the chassis over so that the flaps bend up. Fit the body over the wider part of the chassis, with the flaps inside and the axle holes matching. Brush glue on each flap, and press it against the body until dry. Using transparent tape, tape the body front to the chassis (this area will be concealed by the hood).

7. Fold the hood on the prescored fold lines, and bend it to shape around its attached grille. Tape the butted edges together. Glue the hood flaps to the chassis. Tape the top of the hood to the body front.

8. Test-fit the dowel alignment through each pair of axle holes. You can even up the holes by slicing away any excess board with a craft knife.

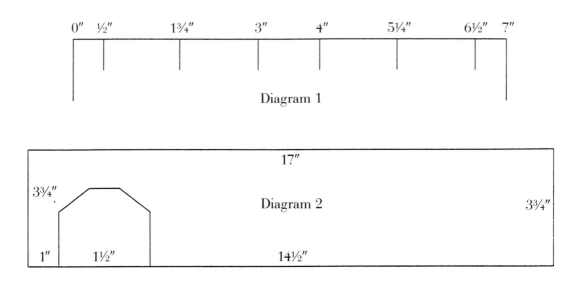

Diagram 1

17"

3¾"

Diagram 2

3¾"

1"   1½"   14½"

TO PAPER THE INTERIOR:

9. Cut a 4½″ × 17″ piece of giftwrap. Use scissors to make ½″-deep clips about ½″ apart along one long edge.

10. Brush glue on the body interior front panel and into the adjoining folds. Set the giftwrap against the gluey area so that the clipped edge extends onto the floor, ¾″ extends beyond the top edge, and ½″ extends onto one side. Smooth the paper in place with your fingers; use a dowel to press it into the crevices. Fold the paper neatly at the lower corners. Repeat to paper each wall of the interior in turn.

11. Make four deep clips in the top extension at each corner. Fold each extension down, and glue it to the body exterior.

12. Cut a 3½″ × 4⅜″ piece of giftwrap. Glue it to the floor of the interior.

TO PAPER THE HOOD:

13. Cut a 4½″ × 7″ piece of red foil giftwrap. Lay it on a flat surface, wrong side up. Mark six points along one 7″ edge, following Diagram 1. Cut a ½″ slit perpendicular to edge at each marked point.

14. Brush glue on the top plane only of the hood. Center the paper on the glued area, foil side up, so that ½″ extends beyond the grille and the slit edge extends onto the body front. Smooth in place. Brush each plane surface of the hood in turn, and glue the paper to it. Glue the excess paper to the chassis underside. Glue the tabs formed by the slits to the body front.

Note: If your fingers get sticky, wash off the glue before continuing. Glue smears that are still wet can be wiped from the foil with a damp washcloth.

15. Brush the outer edges of the grille with glue. Fold the hood paper at the two angled edges, and press it onto the grille. Then fold the top and sides onto the grille. Make neat corners, as if you were wrapping a package.

TO PAPER THE BODY EXTERIOR:

16. Cut a 3¾″ × 17″ piece of red foil giftwrap. Lay this strip on a flat surface, wrong side up, with the long edges at the top and bottom. Trace the grille cover pattern. Place the tracing on the strip 1″ from the left edge and with the lower edges aligned (Diagram 2). Tape down with removable transparent tape. Cut on the solid lines. Remove the tracing paper, and save the foil cutout section.

17. Brush glue onto the front of the body exterior around the hood. Position the strip with the hood opening on it, foil side up, and press in place. Brush glue onto the adjoining car side, and smooth the excess strip on it. Continue until the exterior is papered all around.

18. Turn the car over. Brush the edge of the chassis with glue, and fold the excess paper onto it. Make neat corners, as if you were wrapping a package.

19. Test-fit the grille cutout against the front of the hood. You

may need to trim each edge of the cutout a fraction of an inch to fit the grille without overlapping. Brush the grille with glue, and press the cutout in place. Glue the extension to the underside.

20. Tape the chassis tracing to red foil giftwrap. Cut along the dash lines. Test-fit the piece against the underside of the chassis. Trim if necessary; then glue in place.

TO MAKE THE TIRES:

21. Using a compass, draft twelve 2″-diameter circles on cardboard or posterboard. Reinsert the compass point into one hole, and draw a 1¼″-diameter concentric circle. Repeat three more times. Score all the circles with a craft knife; then cut them out with sharp scissors. You should have eight solid circles and four doughnuts.

22. Trace the actual-size hub pattern. Tape the tracing to one of the solid circles. Use a hole punch to cut the small circles on the pattern. Use this hub as a template to punch the seven remaining solid circles.

23. Brush four of the punched hubs with clear glue. Place the four remaining hubs on top, aligning the punched holes. Let dry.

24. Cut four 3″-square pieces of dark green confectioner's foil. Brush one side of each doughnut with a light coat of glue. Press each doughnut, glue side down, onto the wrong side of the foil. Turn each piece over, and smooth out the foil.

25. Cut eight 3″-square pieces of gold confectioner's foil. Brush both sides of each punched circle with glue, and sandwich between two sheets of foil. Smooth out the foil

with your fingers, pressing gently from both sides to make small depressions at the punched holes. Press the middle to mark the hole made by the compass point.

26. Trim the green foil to within ⅜″ of each inner circle. Clip into the foil every ¼″ to make tabs. Brush the wrong side of each green tire lightly with glue; then fold these tabs to the wrong side. Position each green tire on a gold hub, and hold until glue is set. Trim remaining loose foil to within ⅜″ of the outer circle. Fold it to the wrong side.

TO MAKE THE STEERING WHEEL:

27. Using a compass, draft three 1¼″-diameter circles on cardboard or posterboard. Score with a craft knife, and cut out with sharp scissors.

28. Trace the actual-size steering wheel pattern. Punch holes in all three circles, as you did for hubs in Step 22. Glue the pieces together with the punched holes aligned.

29. Cut two 2½″-square pieces of gold confectioner's foil. Glue the steering wheel between them, sandwich style, and finger-press to accentuate the depressions. Trim the foil a scant ⅛″ beyond the outer rim. Press the excess in to resemble a chocolate-candy coin.

TO ATTACH THE TIRES:

30. Secure the 3¼″ and 4″ dowels in a vise for drilling. Using a 1/16″ bit, drill a ⅜″ hole in each end. Push the dowels into the motorcar axle holes—insert an awl into the drilled hole to help guide the dowel out the other side.

31. Use an awl to bore a small hole in each gold hub. Brush the end of each axle with tacky glue. Slip a brass nail through the hub and into the gluey axle hole. Hold until set.

TO ATTACH THE STEERING WHEEL:

32. Using a coping saw, saw off one end of the 4¼″ dowel at a 45° angle. Cut a 2″ × 4¼″ piece of gold confectioner's foil. Brush the wrong side of the foil with tacky glue, and wrap it around the dowel.

33. Hot-glue the angled end of the dowel to the back of the steering wheel. Stand the steering column upright against the front interior, and hot-glue in place.

TO MAKE THE HORN:

34. Roll a large gumball-sized ball of modelling compound. Mould it over the tapered end of the cake-decorating tip with your fingers to make horn. Bake the horn, including tip, in a 275°F (135°C) oven for 20 minutes, or as suggested in the modelling compound package instructions. Set on a rack to cool.

35. Paint horn bulb black. Reinforce join with hot glue if necessary. Hot-glue horn to motorcar at right of steering column.

FINISHING AND TRIMS:

36. Bend two 15-mm white chenille stems to shape around the top of the car body and trim off excess. Hot-glue in place. Shape the remaining 15-mm chenille stem around the front grille and glue in place. Glue 6-mm white chenille around the body/hood join.

37. Lay the "Merry Christmas" script, wrong side up, on wax paper. Brush lightly with tacky glue. Use tweezers to angle the script on the car body above the tire; then press in place. Repeat to decorate other side.

38. Use tweezers to position stars around the script and on the hood. Affix foil stickers to the grille and rear bumper as car medallions.

TO MAKE THE SACK:

39. Fold 8″ × 8″ wool fabric in half, wrong sides facing, and stitch two side seams. Turn top edge down ⅝″ all around and press. Stitch ⅜″ from folded edge to make casing. Turn to right side. Pick out a few stitches in one side seam to make opening in casing.

40. Make a 12″ twisted cord from green pearl cotton (see box). Draw cord through opening in casing.

FINISHING:

41. Stand Santa in car behind steering wheel. Load back of car with a candy-filled sack, a fir tree, and toys.

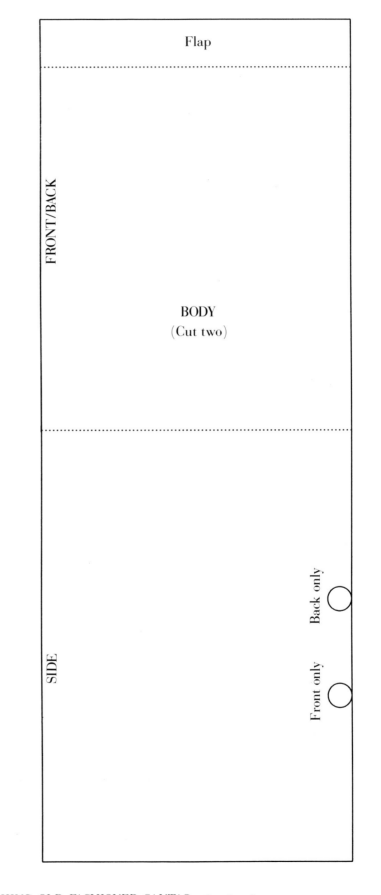

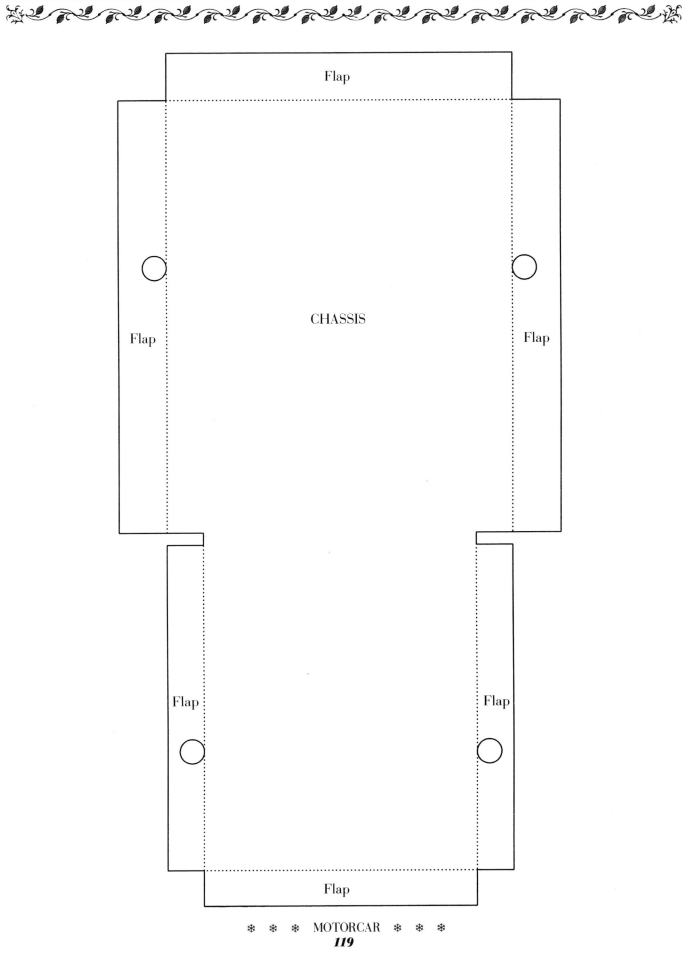

Flap

Flap

CHASSIS

Flap

Flap

Flap

Flap

HUB

GRILLE COVER

STEERING WHEEL

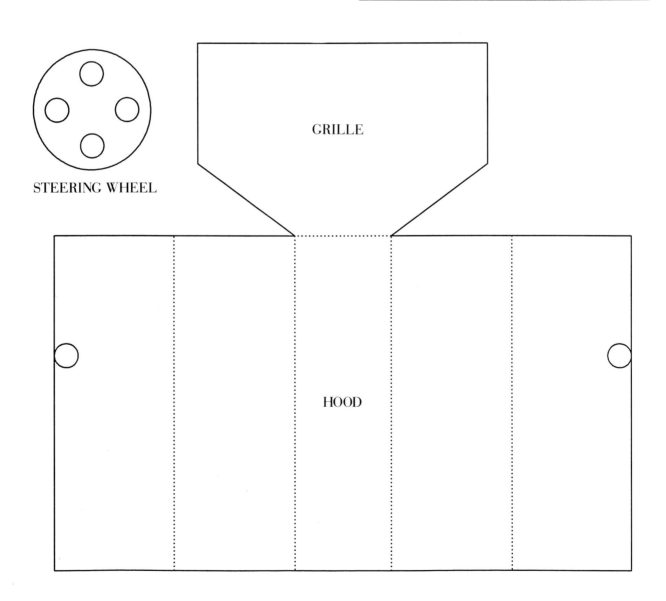

GRILLE

HOOD

NICHOLAS MAN
CANDY CONTAINER

A realistic sticker face brings a handcrafted Nicholas man to life. Modelled after Weihnachtsmann (the Christmas man) made in Germany, this charming fellow is easy to re-create with tea-dyed batting. His red hat is fashioned of paper twist, and the gold buttons are cut from foil doilies. He is shown here topping a round candy container, but he would also make a fetching tree ornament. The Nicholas Man is 8" tall; the candy container with the lift-off lid is 5" across × 2" high.

❋ ❋ ❋ ❋ ❋

NICHOLAS MAN

MATERIALS AND TOOLS

Santa sticker or scrap face, about 1″ across

5″ × 8″ tea-dyed high-loft batting (to tea-dye, see box that follows)

two 12″ 9-mm white chenille stems

5″ red paper twist, unfurled

6″ gold metallic ¼″ trim

gold foil doily

½ yard narrow gold braid or roping

three velvet leaves with berries

thick white tacky glue

rubber cement

stiff brush (for glue)

DIRECTIONS

1. Carefully split the tea-dyed high-loft batting into two layers.
2. Brush the end of one chenille stem for 3½″ with tacky glue. Pull some fibres from the inner surface of the split batt, and wrap them tightly around the glued area, for a diameter of about ⅜″. Repeat to cover other end of same stem. Let dry.
3. Fold the stem in half to make an inverted **V**. Make **L**-shaped bends 1″ from each end to form feet.
4. Cut two 2¼″ × 3″ pants legs from one split-batt piece. Wrap the batt, smooth side out, around each leg, beginning 1″ above the ankle. Arrange and pin so that the 3″-long "seam" is at the back. Grade the seam edge with scissors; then glue pants leg in place.
5. Cut a 7″ length from the remaining chenille stem. Cut one 2″ × 7″ sleeve piece from the split batt. Wrap the sleeve, smooth side out, around the stem. Grade and glue the seam as for pants.

6. Cut one 7″ × 4″ coat from the split batt. Wrap the coat, smooth side out, around the Santa body so that the hem is about 2½″ above the ankles and the seam falls to the right of middle front. Glue in place.
7. Glue the sleeve/arm piece to the back of the coat about 1½″ from the top. Bring the arms together in front. Let dry thoroughly.
8. Hand-sew a running stitch around the top circular edge of the coat. Gather until snug to form the head. Glue on the face about ½″ from the top. Fill in around the face with extra fibre pulled from the remaining split batt as needed.
9. Trace the actual-size hat pattern. Tape the tracing to the unfurled paper twist and cut out. Place the curved section of the hat above the sticker face, and shape it around the head. Overlap the hat edges at the back, and secure with rubber cement. You may need to pad the inside of the hat with extra fibres as you work.
10. Brush the wrong side of the ¼″ trim with tacky glue, and press in place around edge of hat. Cut four small medallions from the gold doily, and glue to coat and hat as

HAT

buttons. Glue leaves in arms.

11. Tie the gold rope around Santa's waist for a belt. Cut a snippet off one end, fray, and glue to tip of hat.

CANDY CONTAINER

MATERIALS AND TOOLS

medium-weight cardboard or 3-ply posterboard

Christmas giftwrap (for lining)

plain newsprint (for exterior)

7" red paper twist, unfurled

white opaque glitter

white sparkling glitter

three old glass Christmas balls

½ yard coordinating 1" ribbon

masking tape

white glue

clear arts-and-crafts glue

rubber cement

hot-glue gun

stiff brush (for glue)

mechanical pencil

transparent ruler

compass

craft knife

wax paper

book or other flat, heavy weight

DIRECTIONS

TO MAKE THE CANDY CONTAINER:

1. Use a compass to draft a 5"-diameter circle (label T for top) and a 4⅞"-diameter circle (label B for bottom) on cardboard or posterboard. Using a transparent ruler and a craft knife, score one 2" × 16¼" strip (label T) and one 2" × 15¾" strip (label B) on cardboard or posterboard. Cut out all four pieces with scissors.

2–4. Same as Feather Tree Candy Containers, Steps 2–4 (page 107). The tabs can be ⅜" instead of ¼". Repeat steps 2–4 with circle T and strip T to make top.

TO LINE CANDY CONTAINER:

5. On printed Christmas giftwrap, draft a 4⅞"-diameter circle (T), a 4¾"-diameter circle (B), a 2½" × 16¼" strip (T), and a 2½" × 15¾" strip (B). Cut out all pieces.

6–8. Same as Feather Tree Candy Containers, Steps 6–8 (page 107). Repeat Steps 7 and 8 with circle T and strip T to line candy container top.

TO PAPER THE CONTAINER EXTERIOR:

9. On plain newsprint, draft a 4⅞"-diameter circle (T), a 4¾"-diameter circle (B), a 3" × 16¼" strip (T), and a 3" × 15¾" strip (B). Cut out all pieces.

10–12. Same as Feather Tree Candy Containers, Steps 10–12 (page 107). Repeat steps 10–12 to paper the container top.

13. Place cover on candy container. Set on wax paper on a flat surface, and lay a second sheet of wax paper on top. Weight with a heavy book overnight or until dry.
Note: to prevent warpage, finish steps 1–13 in one session.

FINISHING:

14. Using the transparent ruler and a mechanical pencil, mark three 2⅛"-wide strips across the unfurled paper twist. Cut apart with scissors. Glue the three strips, end to end, with rubber cement to make one long strip. Let dry.

15. Place the cover on the candy container. Brush the 2"-deep rim with rubber cement. Wrap the long strip around the rim, pressing lightly until it adheres. Trim off the excess; then overlap the ends and cement in place.

16. Position the compass point in the top pinhole (it should be visible from original drafting), and draw a 1½"-diameter circle. Brush the outer "doughnut" with clear arts-and-crafts glue. Sprinkle on a mixture of opaque and sparkling glitter, and press in place lightly with fingertips. Tap off excess.

17. Work out an arrangement for your Santa, glass balls, and ribbon in the "doughnut hole." Secure all pieces to the cover with hot glue.

SCRAPS TRUNK

Lively hand-pasted collages reflect the Victorian passion for collecting and displaying scrap pictures. The "canvases" for this popular art included hat boxes, *folding screens, and even furniture. You can try this picture-making technique on any smooth flat surface. A renovated doll-clothes trunk is especially practical for holding* *holiday mail, party favors, small gifts, or family photos. The trunk shown measures 7½" × 13½" × 7"—a perfect tabletop size.*

❋ ❋ ❋ ❋

MATERIALS AND TOOLS

assorted Santa Claus stickers and scraps

Christmas giftwrap, gift bags, greeting cards, and tags

Christmas motifs cut from calendars, magazines, and similar printed sources

doll-clothes trunk, any size

black high-gloss latex paint

metallic gold oil-based paint or finish

clear oil-based sealer

thick white tacky glue

paintbrushes

stiff brush (for glue)

small sharp scissors

transparent ruler

craft knife

100- or 120-grit sandpaper

small jar or dish

DIRECTIONS

1. If you are refurbishing an old trunk, begin by removing any worn stickers and smoothing the rough surfaces with sandpaper. Wipe clean with a damp cloth.

2. Paint the trunk black and let dry. Restore the hardware by brushing on metallic gold paint. Let dry thoroughly. Brush on clear sealer, taking smooth, even strokes to prevent bubbles from forming. Let dry thoroughly.

3. Use small, sharp scissors to cut out the pictures you have selected from giftwrap and other printed papers. In a small jar or dish, thin some tacky glue with water until it reaches a heavy-cream consistency. Brush mixture on the back of each picture, all the way to the edges. Press the picture in place on the trunk. It is best to glue down large-scale pictures first, and then arrange and overlap smaller pictures around them. Work on one side of the trunk at a time. Keep the trunk closed, and paste the pictures right over the lid opening.

4. When the glue is bone-dry, line up a transparent ruler along the lid "crack" and carefully slit through all the paper layers with a craft knife. The finished trunk can be used as is or brushed with a protective sealer.

TIPS FOR CUTTING SCRAPS

For a crisper look, trim away the excess white margin that appears around some stickers and punch-out scraps. Use small scissors, such as embroidery, manicure, or Scherenschnitte scissors. As you cut, move the paper, not the scissors. For difficult inside angles, cut into the angle from two directions. When using stickers, you'll find it easier to trim first and then remove the peel-off backing.

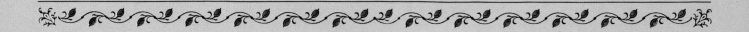

BLOCK PUZZLES

Even adults will find old-fashioned picture-block puzzles a challenge to solve. Popular in the late 1800s, picture-block sets could be rearranged to create six different scenes. For the best results, choose all six pictures from a single source, such as a matte-finish giftwrap or a collection of reproduction postcards. The puzzles shown here measure 6" × 4½" and a postcard-size 3" × 5", but you can add more blocks for puzzles as large as you wish.

* * * * *

MATERIALS AND TOOLS

12 unfinished 1½" wood blocks for large puzzle *or* 15 unfinished 1" wood blocks for small puzzle

paper with printed pictures, such as giftwrap, greeting cards, or postcards

water-based clear matte finish (optional)

thick white tacky glue

stiff brush (for glue)

transparent ruler

craft knife

emery board

self-healing cutting mat

sheet of typing paper

DIRECTIONS

TO MAKE A PAPER WINDOW:

1. If you are using scenic giftwrap, a paper window will help you isolate pictures for your puzzle. Place a sheet of typing paper on a self-healing cutting mat. Set the blocks on top as if the puzzle were assembled (large blocks in four rows of three, small blocks in three rows of five). Lightly trace around the blocks, and then remove them.
2. Draw two diagonal lines from corner to corner to make an **X**. Using a craft knife, cut on the marked **X**, going slightly beyond the corners. Fold back the four triangular flaps to create a rectangular opening that is about ¹⁄₁₆" larger all around than the finished puzzle size.

TO CUT THE PICTURES:

3. To allow for subtle variations in the block dimensions, cut the pictures for each block one at a time. Place the giftwrap sheet on the cutting mat, right side up. Move the paper window around until you find the best view of the picture you want to use. Set up the blocks inside the window, covering the picture. Carefully lift away the window without disturbing the blocks. If you are using a postcard, simply place the blocks on top of the postcard.

4. Hold the craft knife against the top right block (top left if you are left-handed) for cutting. Carefully cut the picture along the block's top and side edges. Remove this block and set it aside, face up. Complete cutting the first picture square by using the two adjacent blocks as a cutting guide. Place this picture square on top of the block you removed. Continue cutting and removing the picture squares and blocks, one by one. Be sure to keep the blocks and squares in order as you remove them.

FINISHING:

5. When all the squares for one picture are cut, glue them onto their corresponding blocks. In a small jar or dish, thin some tacky glue with water until it reaches a heavy-cream consistency. Brush a thin coat of glue onto the face of the block, making sure the edges are moistened. Lay the picture square on top and smooth it out.
6. When the glue is thoroughly dry, use an emery board to sand off the four edges around the picture square for an aged look.
7. Repeat Steps 3–6 until all six sides of each block are papered and sanded. You can protect the papered blocks with a clear matte finish if you desire; test on sample paper first.

INDEX